The
Little
Windows 95
Book

Kay Yarborough Nelson

Peachpit Press

The Little Windows 95 Book

Kay Yarborough Nelson

Peachpit Press
2414 Sixth St.
Berkeley, CA 94710
(510) 548-4393
(510) 548-5991 (fax)

Find us on the World Wide Web at: http://www.peachpit.com

Peachpit Press is a division of Addison-Wesley Publishing Company.

Cover design: **TMA** Ted Mader + Associates

Cover illustration: John Grimes

ISBN 1-56609-181-0

0 9 8 7 6 5 4 3
Printed and bound in the United States of America

The centipede was happy quite
Until a toad in fun
Said, "Pray, which leg goes after which?"
That worked her mind to such a pitch,
She lay distracted in a ditch,
Considering how to run.

Mrs. Edward Craster, in *Cassell's Weekly* (1871)

Contents

Introduction

No matter whether you're an absolute beginner or an old Windows hand, you'll find all sorts of things that are new in Windows 95. It bears no resemblance to the Windows you know, or don't know. In fact, it bears little resemblance to anything on the planet, Macintoshes included, no matter what you've heard.

If you've never seen a Window window, spend your lunch hour with this little book and discover how to use Windows. This book's both concise and irreverent; one or the other, or both, should be appealing.

Never Done Windows Before?

If you've used Windows 3.1 before, you're probably wondering what's different with Windows 95's interface. Basically, everything. You use both mouse buttons now. The File Manager and Program Manager are gone, but you do what they did from all sorts of different places. The Find utility's a mini-File Manager, for example. So are Open and Save As dialog boxes, and utilities named My Computer and the Explorer. Your program groups are on a Start menu. The Close box isn't where you expect it, either. There's a Recycle Bin for deleting files. You can use long file names with spaces in them. A taskbar lets you switch among programs that are running and move between windows. And that's just the beginning.

Just about Everything's New!

Let the fat books rant and rave about preemptive multitasking, 32-bit protected mode, virtual device drivers, and per-process resource tracking. This little book quickly illustrates what makes a difference in how you actually use this new system every day for real work.

Frankly, Windows right out of the box is pretty intimidating—and downright useless if you can't use it. You really have to set it up to work your way. I'll show you how. Watch the tips in the margins.

Get Started I'm assuming that you have Windows 95 installed on your computer and that it's running. You didn't buy this book to read a long introduction, so let's get started with the five-dollar tour. The first and most basic task in Windows 95 is learning where to *find stuff*.

- If you're a beginner, start with Chapter 1.
- If you know your way around Windows 3.1, and if you're bravehearted, start with Chapter 2.

Here's what's in the book:

Chapter 1 A Guided Tour

Chapter 2 Survival Tactics

Chapter 3 Working with Windows

Chapter 4 Exploring Your Files

Chapter 5 Making Windows Work Your Way

Chapter 6 Working with Programs

Chapter 7 Printing

Chapter 8 It's not You, It's...

Appendix A Here's How

Appendix B Keyboard Shortcuts

I'm KayNelson@aol.com, or on CompuServe at 7000,1176@ compuserve.com.

A Guided Tour

1

If you've never done Windows 95 before, this is the place to start. It gives you an overview of where things are and the basics of what to do. The normal startup desktop doesn't give you many clues. All you see are a few icons, depending on how Windows 95 was installed on your computer.

▶ **Tip:** *If you've had experience with Windows and feel more daring, start with Chapter 2.*

A guided tour also comes with Windows 95. To take it, click the Tour button in the Welcome screen. You may not see that Welcome screen, though, if someone has turned it off so it doesn't automatically display any more.

   If you haven't got Windows started, you may want to turn on your computer now so that you can try out some basic techniques during this guided tour.

Getting Started

1

Mousing Around

If you've never used a mouse before, it takes some getting used to, so I'll show you a few tricks before we start.

The mouse pointer is the small solid arrowhead on the screen. As you move the mouse on your real desktop, you'll see the pointer moving on the screen. Try it. Here's the mouse secret: *you can pick it up.* If you've pushed the mouse all the way to the far corner of your (real) desktop and you're just about to knock over your cup of coffee but what you want is just a little farther over on the screen… pick up the mouse and move it nearer to you! The pointer will stay on the screen where you left it. Try it and see.

You use the mouse in three basic ways: by clicking (with both the left and right mouse buttons), double-clicking, and dragging.

▶ **Tip:** *If you're left-handed, you can use the Mouse control panel to switch buttons. You'll see how in Chapter 3.*

Clicking

To select an item on the screen, you can move the mouse pointer to it and click once with the left mouse button. Selecting an item makes it active, so that you can work with it. For example, you click once on a button or a menu command to choose it. Click on the Close button to close the Welcome screen and get it out off your way.

Right-Clicking

You also use the *right* mouse button in Windows 95. Many things you *right*-click on open a pop-up menu. Right-clicking on the desktop brings up one of these menus. Right-clicking on other items displays a "What's This" box that explains what the feature does. I'll use "click" to mean "click with the left mouse button" and "right-click" to mean "click with the right mouse button."

▶ **Tip:** *If something isn't responding the way you think it should, try double-clicking on it.*

Double-Clicking

You can also double-click on some items. To open a folder, for example, you'll need to double-click on it (click twice quickly with the left mouse button).

Dragging

Dragging is a four-step process: click on the item, keep the mouse button down, move the pointer to where you want the item, and release the mouse button. You'll also see it called dragging and dropping. For example, to move a window, drag it by its title bar with the left mouse button.

Windows 95 adds a new dragging technique: right-dragging and dropping (with the *right* mouse button down instead of the left). If you drag an icon with the right mouse button down, for example, you'll see a pop-up menu that lets you move the icon, create a shortcut for it (you'll see what this is soon), or make a copy of it.

You'll get a chance to try out more of these mouse techniques during our tour.

Ready? Now that you've closed the Welcome screen, you're looking at the desktop. You'll be getting a visual and audible clue to click on Start, so go right ahead, and you'll see the Start menu.

The Tour Begins

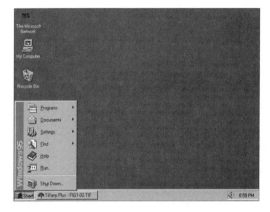

Click Programs to see what Windows 95 programs have been installed on your computer. Yours will be different from mine, depending on what Windows 95 found during installation.

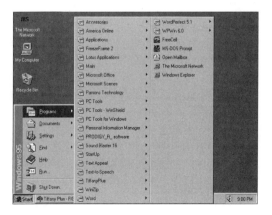

You'll notice that you're getting a series of "sticky" cascading menus that stay open without your having to hold the mouse button down. As you move the mouse pointer over each item, it's highlighted. Just click once to select it. If you move the mouse pointer over any of the items that have an arrowhead next to them, you'll get another menu.

Continuing to explore the Start menu, move the pointer over Documents, and you'll see the last fifteen or so you've worked with. You can click on a document to open it again. If you haven't worked on any documents yet, nothing will be listed here.

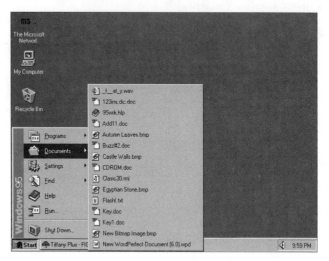

▶ Tip: *You can get Help by pressing F1, too, which is usually faster than using this menu.*

Clicking Settings gives you access to the Control Panel. Here's where your printers are, too, and where you add new printers.

Choosing the next command, Find, takes you to a fairly sophisticated Find facility where you can search for files and even search for text within files. We'll explore it more in Chapter 3.

And the last commands on the Start menu are Help, Run, and Shut Down. In a new-style Windows dialog box, clicking the question mark icon also gets you help.

The Run command lets you start an application if you know the command used to start it, and Shut Down does exactly what you think it does: it lets you turn your computer off or restart it. Don't forget Shut Down!

Now click once on the empty desktop area. The menus will close so you can see the taskbar at the bottom of the screen.

The Taskbar

If you click to start a program running or open a window, you'll see it listed on the taskbar. As you launch applications and open documents, they'll be listed there, and you can switch among them by clicking on their buttons on the taskbar. Here I've started a few programs running.

At the far-right corner of the taskbar, you'll see the system clock. Click on it to see the date. Click on the speaker to adjust the speakers' volume.

That's not all there is to the desktop, but before we go on, you need to see how to manipulate the new-style windows. Try opening a window by double-clicking on your My Computer icon:

Window Basics

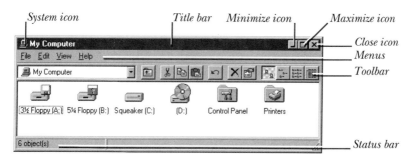

The title bar at the top of the window identifies it. You can tell the active window because its title bar is a different color or intensity than the other windows' title bars.

Only one window can be active at a time.

The Active Window

▶ **Tip:** *To make a window active, just click in it.*

The System Icon

The System menu opens when you click on the System icon in the upper-left corner of the window. (Try it.) This icon is pretty useless for everything except closing the window, because there are better ways to do everything that's listed on its menu. You can just double-click on the System icon to close the window.

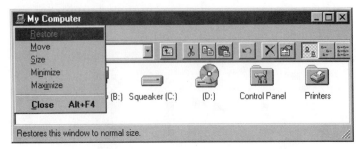

For now, close the menu by pressing Esc. That's a handy way to close a menu without choosing anything from it.

Menus

Just beneath the System icon, you'll see a menu bar. As you click on a menu name and then move the mouse pointer, menus appear. You can click on a command to use it, or just type the letter that's underlined in the command. Click on Help and watch the menu appear; then press Esc or click somewhere outside the menu to close it.

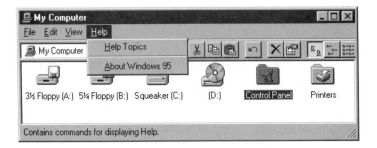

The Toolbar

Under the menu bar, there's a toolbar. If it's not showing on your screen, open the View menu and choose Toolbar. I've closed up the window on the next page to concentrate on the toolbar.

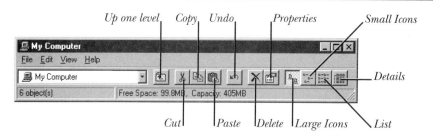

Up one level   _Copy_   _Undo_   _Properties_   _Small Icons_

Cut   _Paste_   _Delete_   _Large Icons_   _List_   _Details_

There's also a status bar at the bottom of the window that gives you information about what's in the window. If you're not viewing the status bar, choose Status Bar from the View menu.

The status bar has a hidden feature: it shows you what menus will do if you choose from them and displays boxes explaining what the mysterious icons are as you move the mouse pointer over them. But you won't get this information if you're not displaying the status bar.

The Status Bar

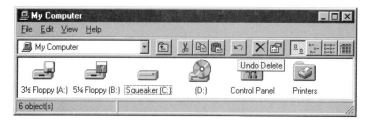

Up in the top-right corner of the window are three tiny icons. The first one minimizes the window. When you minimize a window by clicking on this icon, the window shrinks down to button size and appears on the taskbar. But it's in memory, ready to spring to life again when you click its button on the taskbar.

The Minimize Icon

▶ **Tip:** _All open windows are listed on the taskbar, including any windows that are minimized (open and still in memory but not displayed). When you close a window, its name is removed from the taskbar._

Try it, if you like. Click on My Computer's Minimize icon and watch My Computer appear on your taskbar. Then click that My Computer button to open the window again and watch it come back to the size it was.

The Maximize Icon

▶ **Tip:** *Double-click in a window's title bar to maximize or restore a window. It's faster than trying to hit those tiny icons.*

The middle icon is either the Maximize icon or the Restore icon, depending on whether the window's full-screen size or not. If the window's smaller than full-screen size, click the Maximize icon to make it fill the screen. If the window is already filling the screen, the icon changes to one that looks like two windows stacked on top of each other, and you can click it to shrink the window back to the way it was before you maximized it. Click it a couple of times to see how it works.

The Close Icon

The Close icon is the one with the X. If you used Windows before, you may remember it being on the left. Well, it's over here now. I closed a lot of windows by mistake until I got used to this. If you close the My Computer window by mistake, just double-click on the My Computer icon on your desktop to open it again.

Moving a Window

All you have to do to move a window is drag it by its title bar. Try it: move My Computer to a different place on the screen.

Changing a Window's Size

Now put the mouse pointer at one of the window's bottom corners, and you'll see it change shape to a double arrowhead. Drag the window inward to make it smaller. Try it with your My Computer window.

Scroll Bars

You've made the My Computer window smaller, so you'll probably see a scroll bar. Very often, a window you open can't display everything that's in it. If so, the window will have a scroll bar—either a vertical one along the right side or a horizontal one across the bottom, or both. If a window doesn't have anything hidden that you can't see, you won't see any scroll bars. This one has a horizontal scroll bar.

To see more of what's in a window, click on the arrow on the scroll bar, or drag the scroll bar's scroll box. Or put the mouse pointer on a scroll arrow and hold the mouse button down.

My Computer shows icons for your computer's floppy disk drives and hard drives, plus icons for the Control Panel folder and the Printers folder. If you're on a network, your network drives will also be listed in My Computer.

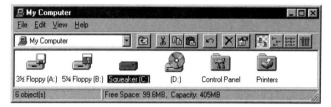

My Computer

▶ **Tip:** *I've named my hard drive. You can name yours, too. Right-click on the drive's icon, choose Properties, and type a name for the drive in the Label box.*

To see what's on your hard drive, double-click on its icon. To see what's on a disk in a floppy drive, double-click on its icon. A new window opens, listing the contents of that disk, with any folders that are there displayed first. You can think of folders as program groups, or as directories, if you've used Windows before. If you haven't, just think of them as file folders. You can put all sorts of things in file folders—programs, documents, other folders, graphic images—just like you'd stuff a real manila folder in a real filing cabinet.

▶ **Tip:** *To see what's in a folder, double-click on it.*

You may think that using My Computer is the only way to navigate around in the folders on your computer, but it's not. There are lots of other ways to get where you're going. My Computer happens to be the easiest thing to *find*, because it's right there on your desktop. But you can fix that easily enough—soon enough.

The Recycle Bin

One more item that may appear on your desktop is the Recycle Bin. It holds all the files you delete until you empty the bin, and that's all you need to know about it for now.

The Games

We can't leave this quick tour without finding the games! They're in the Accessories folder inside the Programs folder on the Start menu. Click Start, then Programs, then Accessories, and pick a game. Tell yourself (and your boss) that it's a way of getting used to the new Windows interface.

Off the Bus! It's Time to Walk

That's not all there is to Windows, but it's the pretty face you see when you start—just the tip of the iceberg. In Chapter 2 you'll see lots more about working with Windows, including more about getting help when you're stuck.

Jumpstarting Windows 95

If you've used Windows 3.1, you're going to be frustrated at first with Windows 95. No longer can you zip around doing what you used to know how to do. Use the survival tactics in this chapter so you can find your way around until you get up to speed with the new Windows.

Survival Tactic #1. Once you find something you use regularly, make a shortcut to it and put it on your desktop. A **shortcut** is a pointer to the actual item that's stored on your hard disk. It isn't really the item itself, so shortcuts don't eat up space on your hard disk. To make a shortcut quickly, press Ctrl+Shift and drag an icon to the desktop; then choose Create Shortcut(s) Here. Then all you need to do to use the program or open the document or folder is double-click on its shortcut on the desktop. Shortcut icons have a little curved arrow on them.

Your desktop will be cluttered for a while. So what. At least you'll be able to find things. Figuring out Windows 95's new filing system is, to say the least, time-consuming.

Here's how to find the basic stuff:

- The Desktop is at the top of the hierarchy. Under it is My Computer.

- The Control Panel folder is in My Computer.

- The Printers folder, which holds icons for all the printers you install, is in My Computer.

- Your hard and floppy drives are listed in My Computer.

The Basic Rules

▶ **Tip:** *If you're making a shortcut of a program, you can just drag its icon to the desktop, and Windows 95 will automatically make a shortcut to it.*

▶ **Tip:** *Instead of using the Start menu to start frequently used programs, put shortcuts to them on your desktop. Shortcuts are much faster than menus.*

Everything else you're looking for in Windows 95 is somewhere on your hard disk in your Windows 95 folder, which has many subfolders.

- Your programs are in a folder called Programs in your Windows 95 folder.
- The games are in the Accessories folder inside the Programs folder.
- The multimedia stuff is also in the Accessories folder.
- System Tools (ScanDisk, Backup, Disk Defragmenter, and so forth) are in the System Tools folder in the Accessories folder.
- Anything that's starting up automatically when you start Windows 95 is in the StartUp folder inside the Programs folder.

Actually, if you follow Survival Tactic #1, you'll probably be able to work with Windows 95 a long, long time without having to learn much else.

Survival Tactic #2. Use the Explorer instead of My Computer. It's easier to see the filing system in the Explorer than in My Computer because the left pane lists folders and the right pane shows their contents. To get to the Explorer easily, right-click on the Start button and choose Explore.

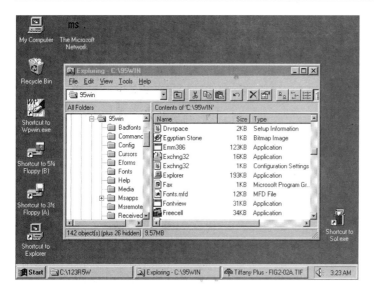

To find the Explorer and make a shortcut to it, look in My Computer and find your Windows folder. Double-click on it and scroll down past the folders to the files. The Explorer's called Explorer. Drag it to the desktop.

Survival Tactic #3. As soon as you get used to the filing system, set up your Start menu the way you want it. All you have to do to add a program to the Start menu is drag its icon to the Start button. You can put documents and folders on your Start menu, too. Windows 95 automatically makes shortcuts to them.

To take something off your Start menu, open the Start Menu folder and drag the item out. They're all shortcuts. You aren't deleting anything.

Survival Tactic #4. Don't be scared to experiment. Right-click on everything to see what effect it has. Many things you *right*-click on (click with the right mouse button) in Windows 95 open a short menu. Here are just a few:

▶ **Tip:** *Alt-double-click on an icon to open its property sheet.*

- Right-clicking on a disk's icon lets you format the disk, for example.

- Right-clicking on a document lets you QuickView it, cut it, or copy it. Right-clicking on the desktop and choosing Properties lets you set screen saver options and choose wallpaper.

- Right-clicking in a title bar opens the window's System menu.

- Right-clicking and dragging an icon on the desktop lets you create a copy or shortcut of it.

- Right-clicking items in a dialog box displays a "What's This" box that explains what the feature does.

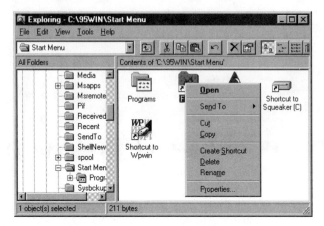

Survival Tactic #5. Get Help frequently. You can press F1 to get help. After that, it's pretty self-explanatory. But once you're within the Help system, the real trick to getting help is to click the Find tab and let Windows search text *within* Help topics. This is the most accurate and usually fastest way to find out all sorts of things, unless you know the name of the index entry you're looking for. And you won't at first.

Survival Tactic #6 Read this book, especially the tips in the margins. Windows 95 gives you all sorts of different ways to do everything. I'm not telling them all, just giving the ones that are easiest and fastest.

Look in the back of the book for all the keyboard short-cuts. There are lots of new ones. Pressing F10 puts you in menu mode, for example. Pressing Shift+F10 opens a selected item's property sheet.

There are those you might expect, too: Alt+Enter opens a property sheet, just as Alt+Enter displayed the Properties dialog box in Windows 3.1. Ctrl+Esc brings up the Start menu, just as Ctrl+Esc opened the Task List in Windows 3.1.

Rule #7. Don't get carried away with long file names.
Think twice before you rethink file names. You can use spaces and lots of characters now, but many of your programs won't be able to recognize the new-style long file names. All your files named My Letter to Aunt Mary in August and My Letter to Aunt Mary in September will appear as mylett~1 and mylett~2 to those programs.

To get used to the new system, view Details in the Explorer and My Computer so you can see the old-style file names. Choose Options from the View menu and uncheck the Hide MS-DOS file extensions box so you can see the extensions. They haven't gone away; they're just not displayed! You may also want to check the Display the full MS-DOS path in the title bar box.

Rule #8 Rethink Windows.

- Think of the Explorer/My Computer as the File Manager.

- Think of the Start menu as the Program Manager.

- Think of sending to the Recycle Bin as deleting.

- Think of the taskbar as the Task List.

- Think of folders as directories.

- Think of everything as an object that has properties you can adjust.

- Think of the right mouse button! And use it.

These tactics will get you through the worst of it. The hardest part is finding things. Skim through Chapter 3, which is about Windows basics. Pay attention to Chapter 4, about My Computer and the Explorer. Check out Chapter 5 for how you can customize Windows 95 to your liking.

Go for It

Working with Windows

This chapter's going to be about the different ways you can manage windows in Windows 95. The system gives you a choice of all sorts of ways for doing all sorts of tasks, but when you're just starting out, you might as well learn a couple of simple ways for the basic stuff and stick to those until you're a lot more experienced with whipping around in Windows 95.

Starting and Exiting Windows

First things first. You normally don't have to worry about starting Windows, because it starts when you start your computer. However, exiting's another matter. Don't just turn off your computer. Choose Shut Down from the Start menu and wait until you get the message that it's safe to turn off the computer.

▶ **Tip:** *If you have trouble starting Windows, see Chapter 8.*

Opening and Closing Windows

You'll be opening and closing windows in Windows a lot. The quickest way to open one is to double-click on its icon. You can also highlight an icon and press Enter to open it.

If the window is represented by a button on the taskbar, just click once there to open it.

To close a window, you have several options:

- If you've got the mouse in your hand, the fastest way is either to double-click on the window's System icon or click once on the Close box in the top-right corner.
- If your hands are on the keyboard, pressing Alt-F4 is probably faster.

If the window is represented by a button on the taskbar, right-click on it and choose Close, or press Alt+F4.

Need Help?

▶ **Tip:** *Get help on how to use Help in Help by double-clicking How To and then double-clicking Use Help.*

One of the other most basic skills you'll need in Windows 95 is how to get help when you're stuck. To be able to get help efficiently, you'll need to know how to use menus and dialog boxes and maneuver through windows, so we'll cover those things as well in this chapter, in a little more detail than in the fifty-cent tour in Chapter 1.

The fastest way to get help is to press F1 instead of choosing Help from a menu. That takes you directly to the Contents tab in Help. Double-click on a closed book to open it and see the Help topics listed in it. Then double-click on a topic to go to it.

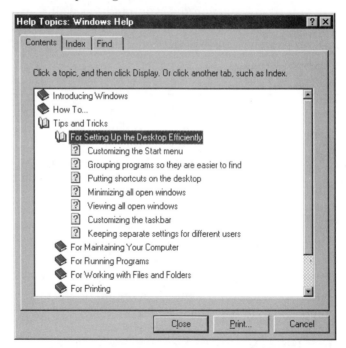

A more efficient way to get help, once you're in the Help system, is to click the Index tab and type the first few letters of the word you're looking for help on. Then double-click on the highlighted topic to read about it.

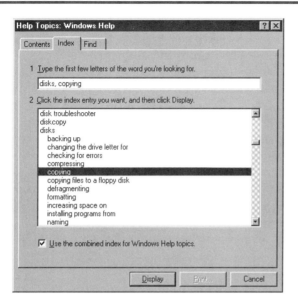

But what if you don't know the name of what you need help on? In that case, click the Find tab and enter *something* about the topic. You'll see some words to help you narrow the search. Click on one of those to see topics about it. Then click on a possibly interesting topic and click the Display button to read about that topic.

▶ **Tip:** *To close the Help system, just press Esc.*

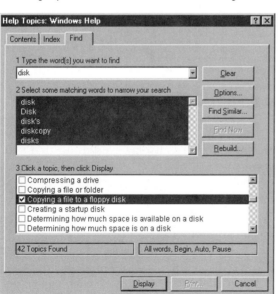

If that topic isn't the one you want, choose Help Topics to get back to where you were, or Back to look at the last topic you looked up in the Help system. Either way lets you move through the help system's screens and branch to different topics. Also, if you see a Related Topics button in a help screen, click on it to get more information.

More Help

Dialog boxes and property sheets often ask you to supply information, which you often don't have. Look at the top-right corner of the dialog box, and you'll usually see a ?. Click it and then click on the item you need help about. A box pops up and describes what the item is.

Interactive Help

Sometimes you'll see a little curved arrow in Help topics. When you click on that arrow, you'll be taken directly to the part of the system where you need to do something.

If there's more to a help screen than can fit in one window, you can scroll to it, as you'll see now.

Moving in a Window

A window can't always display everything that's in it. On the bottom and right sides of a window that contains more than what's showing, you'll see a scroll bar. If a window doesn't have anything hidden that you can't see, you won't see any scroll bars. Scroll bars are always an indication that there's something more to see.

▶ **Tip:** *Watch for horizontal scroll bars at the bottom of the screen. There are lots of them in Windows 95.*

To scroll down to see what's hidden, click in the lower part of the scroll bar. Or click on the small empty box in the scroll bar and drag it down. To move backward to the beginning of the text, click in the upper part of the scroll bar, or drag the empty box up. You can also move the mouse pointer to the boxes with the up and down arrows, and press and hold the left mouse button down to scroll up or down.

Another quick way to scroll horizontally through a wide window is select one item in it and then drag it to the lower-right edge of the window. You'll see the pointer turn to a "No Way" sign, but the window will scroll. Releasing the mouse button puts the item back where it came from.

To move through a window or document one screen at a time, click *just above* the scroll arrow at the bottom of the scroll bar. You can move up screen by screen, too. Click just under the arrow at the top of the scroll bar.

Moving Screen by Screen

A quick way to move through a long window or document is to click in the scroll bar at just about the place where you want to go. To go to the end of the document, click at the end of the scroll bar. Click in the middle to go to the middle. You get the idea.

Relative Scrolling

▶ **Tip:** *Press Ctrl+Z if you move an item to a different folder by mistake. Ctrl+Z is Undo.*

You can use the PgUp and PgDn keys to scroll, too. Press Home to go to the top of a window or End to go to the end.

Scrolling with the Keyboard

Learn about menus here, and you know about them in all your Windows programs. Working with one Windows program is very similar to working with another, because you use the same basic methods for issuing commands.

Using Menus

The menus you see on the menu bars depend on what's in the window. When you click on a menu choice in the menu bar (or press Alt and type the underlined letter), you'll get a pull-down menu.

▶ **Tip:** *You'll get a File menu and an Edit menu in all Windows programs, but the rest of the menus may be different.*

You can select a choice from a pull-down menu by:

- Clicking on it.

- Typing the letter that's underlined (either lowercase or uppercase will do).

- Typing the shortcut keys listed to the right of the option.

Sometimes combining keyboard shortcuts can save you several mouse operations. For example, pressing Alt-F and then typing **O** is a shortcut for selecting File from the menu bar and then choosing Open.

If a menu choice is gray, you can't select it. If there's a check mark next to it, it means that the choice is always either on or off, and it's on. (Selecting it again will turn it off.) If there's an arrowhead next to an item, selecting it will bring up another menu. If there's an ellipsis (…), selecting that choice will bring up a dialog box.

To close a menu without selecting anything from it, press Esc, or click somewhere else. To close a bunch of cascading menus all at once, press Alt+Esc.

Keyboard Shortcuts

Sometimes it's faster not to use the menus at all! Many common menu commands have keyboard shortcuts that you can use instead of opening the menu.

After you work with Windows for a while, you'll probably memorize most of the shortcuts for what you do most often. A lot of them aren't on the menus, but you'll see what those are as we go along. Here are the most common ones. These are listed on the menus and are the same in almost all Windows programs. Memorize them when you get a chance:

Ctrl+A   Select All

Ctrl+C   Copy

Ctrl+V   Paste

Ctrl+X   Cut

Ctrl+Z   Undo (think of the Undo wiZard)

A big chart at the back of the book lists all the hot-key shortcuts, so if you need to look one up, you'll find them all in one place.

Dialog Boxes and Property Sheets

Dialog boxes and property sheets, which are a special type of dialog box, appear all over Windows 95, so you'll need to figure out how to use them.

Dialog boxes come up to ask for some other information that the program needs, or to verify that you really want to carry out a command. Property sheets allow you to customize how an item behaves. To display an icon's property sheet, right-click on it and choose Properties, or press Alt and double-click on it.

When you see a dialog box, you'll need to fill it out with the correct information (how you do this depends on what kind of a box it is) and then press Enter or click OK.

To back out of a dialog box without changing anything, you have a wide range of options. You can click Cancel, press Esc, press Alt+F4, or click its Close box. Stick with Esc to bail out; it works for almost anything.

▶ **Tip:** *Quick selecting: Type the underlined letter to go straight to an item in a dialog box.*

List Boxes

You can scroll through list boxes with the scroll bars. When you see what you want, click on it to highlight it. To choose from a list box without using the mouse, press Alt plus the underlined letter of what you want to choose and scroll with the PgDn and PgUp keys or the arrow keys. When what you want is highlighted, press Enter.

▶ **Tip:** *In some lists you can choose several items by Ctrl-clicking on each one.*

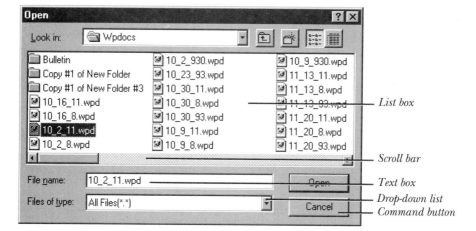

Drop-Down Lists

To choose an item in a drop-down list, click on the down arrow, and you'll see the list appear. Then click on your choice.

To use the keyboard instead of the mouse, type Alt plus the underlined letter of the appropriate selection (such as the n in File name) and then press the down arrow key to open this list box. You can scroll with the arrow and PgUp and PgDn keys. When what you want is highlighted, press Enter.

Text Boxes   If the dialog box has a text box in it, you'll usually need to type information the program needs, such as what file you want to open. First, click in the text box; then type the information. The insertion point is indicated by an I-beam. You can use the regular editing keys, like Backspace, to correct any errors you make as you type. You can also select text by dragging over it.

In some dialog boxes, such as Open dialog boxes, whatever you choose from the list appears in the text box, so you can select with the mouse instead of type.

Command Buttons   Command buttons, like OK and Cancel, are square. If a command button has a bold outline around it, you can press Enter to select it.

In some dialog boxes, you can just double-click on a button to choose it and close the dialog box with the OK button. This is one area in Windows where everything doesn't always work the same way, though. Try double-clicking to see if this will work in your dialog box.

Check Boxes   You use check boxes to turn a feature off (not checked) or on (checked). Click with the mouse to check or uncheck something. Without a mouse, the space bar toggles the check mark on and off.

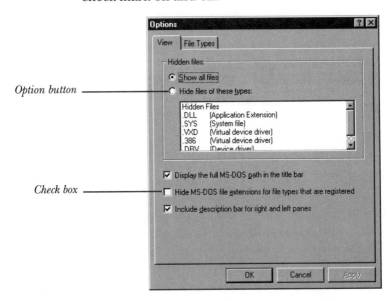

Option buttons are round. Only one option button in a group can be selected. Click on the one you want to choose it. To deselect an option, click on another one.

Without a mouse, press Tab to get to the button you want. A dashed line will surround it when you can choose it. Then press the space bar to select it.

Option Buttons

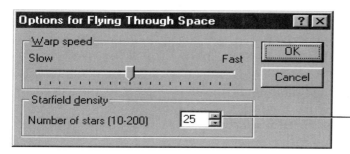

Click here to change settings

Sometimes you'll see a set of up and down arrowheads next to dialog box choices. They indicate that you can change a setting by clicking on the arrows. Click the up arrow to increase the setting; click the down arrow to reduce it.

There are also slider bars that you can drag to change a setting. For samples of all sorts of dialog box controls, right-click on the desktop and choose Properties. You'll have a lot of fun changing colors and screen savers and learning all about dialog box controls.

Some dialog boxes, especially property sheets, have tabs. Chick on a tab to open that part of the property sheet. If you'd rather use the keyboard, press Tab till you get the selection marquee on the current tab; then press Ctrl+Tab to go to the next tab.

Tabs

As you work with Windows, your screen can get cluttered very quickly. Here are a few basic techniques you can use to arrange the windows on your desktop so that you can see what's in them.

Arranging Windows and Icons

The easiest way to move a window is to drag it by its title bar. Click with the mouse in the title bar and, still holding the mouse button down, drag the window where you want it. Let go of the mouse button.

Moving Windows

> **Tip:** *You can move anything that has a title bar. That includes dialog boxes and property sheets: just drag them by their title bars. This is handy if a big dialog box is in the way of something you need to read on the screen.*

The System menu (the one under the little icon in the upper-left corner of the window) also has a Move command. You can choose Move and then press the arrow keys on the keyboard to move the window, pressing Enter when you've got it where you want it, but don't bother with the Move command. It's faster just to drag the window by its title bar.

Resizing Windows

You may also want to make a window smaller or larger. Again, this is a job for the mouse.

Move the mouse to one of the borders of the window. You'll see the pointer change shape to a two-headed arrow. (If it doesn't change shape, that window isn't active. Click in the window to make it active. The active window has a dark title bar.)

When the pointer changes shape, press the mouse button down and drag the window in the direction you want to go—outward to enlarge it, or inward to make it smaller. For example, to shrink a window down to a smaller box in both directions, put the mouse pointer on one of the window's corners (it will change to the double arrowhead here, too) and drag it inward.

> **Tip:** *Quick sizing: drag a window's lower-right corner.*

Click here and drag

Maximizing and Minimizing Windows

The Maximize and Minimize icons in the upper-right corner of a window shrink the window down to a button on the taskbar or enlarge it to full-screen size. Minimizing a window when you're temporarily through working with it is a good idea because it keeps your screen from becoming too cluttered. You can just click on its button on the taskbar to make it bigger when you're ready for it again.

System icon   Minimize icon Maximize icon

Close box

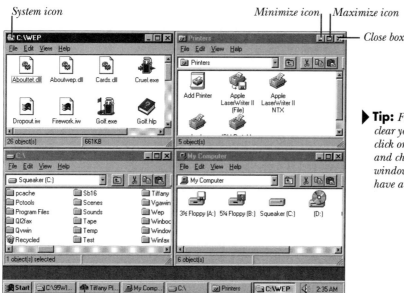

▶ **Tip:** *For a quick way to clear your desktop, right-click on the taskbar and choose Minimize all windows. Instantly, you'll have a clean desktop.*

Keep in mind that minimizing a window isn't the same as closing it! When you close a window, the program is removed from memory. When you minimize a window, it's still in memory, ready to use, just out of your way.

There's also a Restore icon that you'll only see when a window is full-screen size. You'll find out soon enough that you can't resize the window when it's filling the screen! Instead, double-click in its title bar or click the Restore icon (it's the two-window icon in the upper-right corner of the screen) or click the System icon and choose Restore. Any of these ways will restore the window to less-than-full-screen size. Try this now, before you forget it and go crazy (I did the first time I saw it).

If you don't want to arrange Windows by hand (or by mouse), you can use the built-in Tile and Cascade commands. You can see them if you right-click on a blank area on the taskbar. If you choose Tile Horizontally, the open windows will become smaller to fit across your desktop. Tile Vertically stacks them up and down.

▶ **Tip:** *To make a window full-screen size, just double-click in its title bar. It's a lot easier to hit that fat title bar than to hit those tiny icons. Double-click again to restore it to the size it was.*

Arranging Windows

Tiling windows

Choosing Cascade arranges the windows so that only their title bars are showing, except for the window on top.

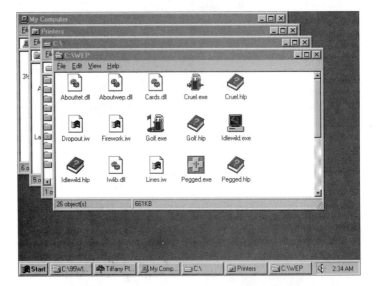

Cascading windows

You'll find that tiling windows is useful if you're copying or cutting and pasting material between several different windows, because you can see more of what you're cutting or copying and where it's supposed to go. Cascading is useful if you're working in only one window at a time but have several windows open and want to be able to see their title bars so that you click to make another one active.

If you don't like the window arrangement, pressing Ctrl+Z undoes it and puts the windows back the way they were, as long as you haven't done anything else in the meantime.

If a window has a View menu, you can have Windows arrange its icons the way you want them. Your choices depend on what sort of window you're looking into.

Arranging Icons

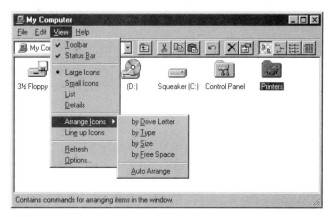

Choosing Auto Arrange simply makes it impossible for you to drag icons into an any-old-way arrangement. You'll find that Auto Arrange can drive you nuts, unless you're *very* tidy.

Each time you open a window, it's listed on the taskbar until you close it. Clicking on its name on the taskbar opens it again. You can cycle among these windows by pressing Alt+Esc or Alt+Tab. The difference is that Alt+Esc selects the buttons on the taskbar and the open windows one by one, while Alt+Tab shows you a box in the middle of the screen listing the open applications and folders one by one.

Alt+Tab is easier to use because you can see what's going on. Keep Alt down and press Tab repeatedly. When you see the window you want to switch to listed, release the Alt key.

Switching between Windows

Here's How

To	Do
Start Windows 95	Turn on your computer.
Exit from Windows	Click the Start button and choose Shut Down.
Open a window	Double-click on its icon or press Enter when the icon is highlighted.
Close a window	Double-click on its System icon, click its Close box, or press Alt+F4.
Get help	Click on Help on the menu bar, press Alt+H, or press F1. If you see a question mark in a dialog box, click on it and then move the pointer to the item you need help about.
Move through a window	Drag or click in the scroll bars, or click on the arrows. Or press Pgp and PgDn.
Select from menus	Click on the item or press Alt and type the underlined letter or number. When the menu appears, click on the item, or type the underlined letter or number. You can also highlight the name with the arrow keys and press Enter, or use a keyboard shortcut if one is available.
Move within a dialog box	Click in it, or press Tab to move forward or Shift+Tab to move backward.
Choose an item in a dialog box	Click on the selection, or type Alt+*letter* (where *letter* is the letter in the box).
Choose several items in a list (sometimes)	Ctrl-click on them.
Choose a command button	Click on it or press Enter.
Choose an option button or check box	Click on it or move to it and press the space bar.

To	Do
Scroll a list dialog box	Click on the up or down arrow in the scroll box, click within the scroll box itself, or type Alt+*letter* and then press the down arrow key.
Move a window	Drag it by its title bar.
Size a window	Drag it outward or inward by its corner.
Maximize a window	Double-click in its title bar or click its Maximize icon.
Minimize a window	Click its Minimize icon.
Restore a window	Double-click in its title bar or click its Restore icon.
Tile windows	Right-click on the taskbar and choose Tile Horizontally or Tile Vertically.
Cascade windows	Right-click on the taskbar and choose Cascade.
Switch between windows	Click in the window, or click its name on the taskbar. Or press Alt+Tab or Alt+Esc.

Exploring Your Files

Instead of the File Manager that the earlier versions of Windows had, Windows 95 provides *two* File Managers: one's called My Computer, and you normally see it right there on your desktop. The other's called the Explorer, and it's a little handier than My Computer. It lets you see the structure of your filing system at a glance. But My Computer's the one most folks see first and wind up using, which is a pity. I'll show you how to use the Explorer, too.

Both the Explorer and My Computer simplify file management by reducing it to copying, cutting, and pasting files from one folder to another. They also let you locate files and folders, rename them, delete them, create shortcuts for them, start programs running, open documents, and print them. And other stuff, too.

The basic difference between My Computer and the Explorer is that the Explorer has two panes: You see your filing system in the left pane and the actual files and folders in the right pane. When you click on a folder in the left pane, its contents appear in the right pane. When you double-click on a folder in the right pane, its contents replace what was there before. Look on the next page.

▶ **Tip:** *Spend some time in this chapter. The Explorer and My Computer are the heart of Windows.*

My Computer vs. the Explorer

Toolbar

The Explorer

Folder list

Status bar

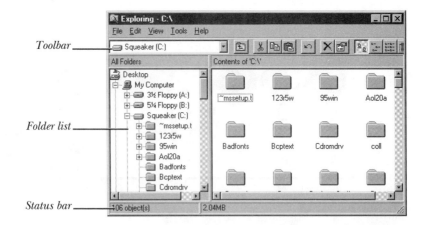

In My Computer, you see drives, folders, and files in one window. When you double-click on a drive or folder, you open a new window. You can just keep going... and going... and going until your desktop is littered with windows. It's all double-clicking in My Computer; single-clicking doesn't do anything.

Toolbar

My Computer

Status bar

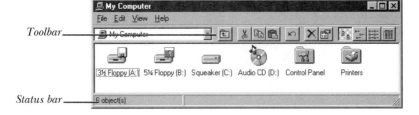

In addition, the Explorer has a Tools menu with a handy Go To command on it as well as a Find command. These differences are subtle, but they can be very annoying unless you're aware of the fact that My Computer and the Explorer *do* work differently. Pick one or the other to use regularly so that you don't go crazy. Both of them work pretty much the same except for these subtleties.

▶ **Tip:** *Or make one work more like the other. See page 40.*

A Little Background

Just in case you're coming to Windows 95 as an absolute computer beginner, here's a little background information about your computer's filing system. Windows 95 tries to "protect" you from it, but you'll often need to know it anyway.

Everything on your computer—what you create and save as well as the programs that are already there—is stored as a *file*. There are different kinds of files, and they're identified by their name—but Windows 95 normally doesn't show you all of their name.

Program files have a (usually invisible) .COM or .EXE after them, like Windows.exe. (These three characters are called an *extension* because they're an addition to the file name. They can help identify what kind of file it is.) Files like these are executable programs. You can run the program, but you can't see what's inside the file.

Document files can contain text, graphics, spreadsheet data, or what have you. These are the files you create by using programs. They may have all sorts of extensions, like .XLS for an Excel spreadsheet, or .DOC for a Word document, or even no extension at all (WordPerfect, for example, doesn't require any extension).

There are also other files that certain programs need, like printer and system files. These, too, have all sorts of extensions. You usually can't see what's in them (if you see anything, it'll be garbage).

Now here's the thing: Windows 95 tells you that you don't have to worry about the extension, and most of the time you don't. In fact, it says that you can use long file names (up to 255 characters). But don't. The reason is that all your old programs don't know about long file names yet, and in the background, hidden where you can't see it, Windows 95 is automatically converting your long file names to old-style eight-characters-plus-a-three-character-extension names. The long file names are really for display, to make things easier for you. Sometimes it helps to know what's going on, though.

Here are the rules for using long file names in Windows 95:

- You can use as many as 255 characters, including spaces. Practically speaking, keep file names under 20 characters so you can see them on the screen without having to scroll.

- You can see upper- and lowercase characters exactly as

File Names

▶ **Tip:** *If you're already familiar with file names, long file names, and path names, just skip to later in the chapter.*

▶ **Tip:** *To tell Windows to let you view extensions, choose Options from My Computer's or the Explorer's View menu, click the View tab, and uncheck the Hide MS-DOS file extensions box.*

Long File Names

▶ **Tip:** *Use these with caution until most of your programs are designed specifically to let you use them.*

you enter them; the system doesn't automatically convert them to all caps or all lowercase.

- You can use + = [ ] and the comma, which you couldn't do before, but you can't use these: \ / : , ; * ? " < > |

The big thing to remember is that if you use long file names (those that exceed the "8.3" convention), enclose them in double quotation marks. For example, to specify the location of a document named Aunt Ora's Letter in your Letters folder, you'd type **"c:\letters\"Aunt Ora's Letter"**.

Files and Folders On your computer, files are organized into a system of folders, which you may remember as directories if you used an earlier version of Windows. Think of a folder as a real file folder in your filing cabinet. You can put all kinds of things in a folder—programs, different documents, graphics, whatever you like. Folders can even hold other folders, just as you stuff folders inside other folders in a filing cabinet.

At this point, you're probably wondering how Windows (and you) can keep track of where things are, if you've got folders within folders within folders. Well, that's where the **path name** comes in. The path is just a list of all the folders that lead to the folder that contains the file that you're looking for, like the house that Jack built. What's confusing about the path name is the cryptic notation used to write it out. Each folder name is separated with a backslash, so C:\Windows\Letters is the path to a folder named Letters under the Windows directory on drive C:.

Now you know more than you probably wanted to. Windows doesn't normally show you path names, either, but you'll discover soon enough that you need to know about the—if you try to use the Run command on the Start menu, for example.

Back to the good stuff.

If you want to use the Explorer, do this now: make a short-cut to the Explorer and put it on your desktop.

- Double-click on My Computer.
- Double-click on the icon of your hard drive.
- Find your Windows directory. It's probably named Windows. Double-click on its icon.
- Find Explorer.
- Drag it to the desktop.

You've made a shortcut to the Explorer. Now you can just double-click on that icon to go there.

Both My Computer and the Explorer let you display a status bar and a toolbar, and both of them are handy. The status bar shows how many objects are in the window as well as their cumulative size, and the toolbar has useful icons for cutting, copying, and viewing files.

Do this now, if your toolbar and status bar aren't showing:

- Choose Toolbar from the View menu.
- Choose Status bar from the View menu.

Each should have a check mark next to them on the menu.

Once you're displaying both of these, you can move the mouse pointer over the icons on the toolbar to get a message about what each of them does. The first icon takes you up one level in the folder structure, the second is Cut, next is Copy, then Paste, followed by Undo, Delete and Properties. The rest control how you view your files and folders.

Make Yourself an Explorer Shortcut

▶ **Tip:** *To really get Windows 95 working for you, you'll need to customize it like we're doing here.*

Deciphering the Window

▶ **Tip:** *You can also go to the Explorer by right-clicking on the Start button and choosing Explore.*

Up one level   Copy   Undo   Properties   Small Icons

Exploring - C:\95WIN

File Edit View Tools Help

95win   All Folders   Contents of 'C:\95WIN'   *Details*

168 object(s)   10.1MB   Undo Move   *List*

Cut   Paste   Delete   Large Icons

Large Icons shows easily readable icons, but no details. It's probably the most useless view, but that's what Windows 95 comes with. You can change it so that you get more information.

37

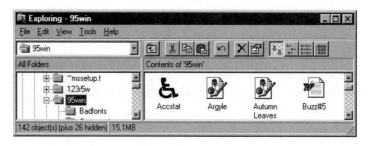

Do this now:

- Click the Details icon so that you can see how big your files are, what type they are, and when they were created.

- Choose Options from the View menu and *uncheck* the Hide MS-DOS files extensions box. You really will often need to see a file's extension, even though Windows 95 pretends that you won't.

- Then (my personal preference, but it's up to you), *check* the Display full MS-DOS path in the title bar. I like to see where I am.

- Click OK.

Now you've got a more useful display.

Path name ⟶
Viewing details
File extensions ⟶

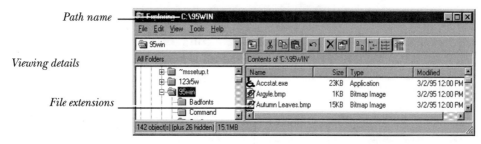

Useful how, you might ask? Well, for one thing, you can see the files you worked with most recently. All you have to do is click on the Modified button, and the files are arranged in a most-recent-first order.

Folders are usually listed first, before any files. Click on the Name button again to bring the files to the top of the list, before any folders in that folder, but listed in reverse alphabetic order.

Here's another trick. See the downward-pointing arrow next to whatever's listed at the top of the left-hand pane, on the toolbar? Click on it, and you'll see the structure of your computer at a glance, which is a handy way of checking where you are when you're several folders down. You can go to any other folder by clicking on it.

▶ **Tip:** *To change the size of the Explorer's panes, drag the bar between the two windows. This makes it easier to see more of the contents of a folder that has lots of files in it.*

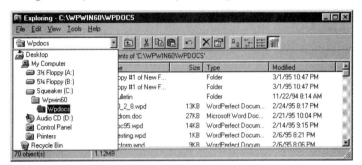

Look closely, and you'll see tiny minuses and pluses next to the Explorer's folders in the left-hand pane. A plus indicates that there are more folders to see in that folder. A minus means the folder is open. Just click on a folder to open or close it, or press the + and - keys on the numeric keypad when the folder's selected.

Looking at Your File Structure

▶ **Tip:** *Home takes you to the top of the list, and End takes you to the end.*

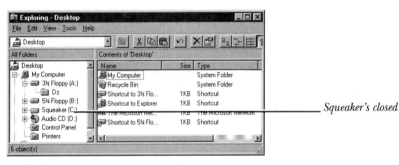

Squeaker's closed

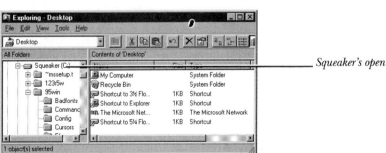

Squeaker's open

You can collapse the whole display and see what's on your desktop by double-clicking on the Desktop icon at the beginning of the list of folders in the left-hand window. Double-click on the Desktop icon again to expand the display. Or select the drive and press the + on the numeric keypad to expand the whole display on the left. Use the - on the numeric keypad to collapse the display.

More Basic Navigation

▶ **Tip:** *In My Computer, shift-click on a folder window's Close button to close that folder and all the open folders that you opened to find it.*

In My Computer, the navigation tricks are easy to remember, because you simply click in an open window to go back to it and double-click on a folder to open it. Here's another trick: pressing Backspace (or clicking that little folder icon on the toolbar) takes you up one level in your folder system.

In the Explorer, the Backspace shortcut works, too, and the Explorer also has a couple of handy navigation aids on its Tools menu:

▶ **Tip:** *Don't worry about wildcards when you use Find, if you know about them. Just type what you're looking for. Even a partial name will do.*

• Choose Find from the Tools menu (or press F3), choose Files or Folders, and enter a file or folder's name to find it. Make sure the Look in box displays the name of your hard drive if you want to search the whole drive. Click Find Now. You can then go to whatever's been found by double-clicking on it.

▶ **Tip:** *In My Computer, you can choose whether you want one window open at a time. Choose Options from the View menu and click the Folder tab.*

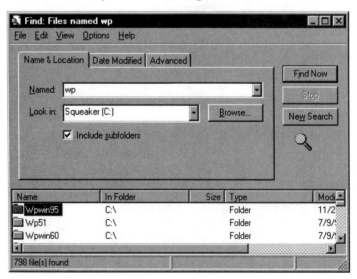

- Choose Go To from the Tools menu, type in the path to the folder or file you want to go to, and click OK. This is faster, but you have to know the path name.

▶ **Tip:** *Ctrl+G is the shortcut for Go To.*

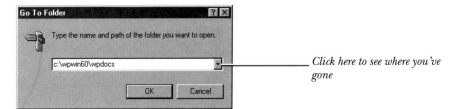

Click here to see where you've gone

You can click on the downward-pointing arrow next to that text box in the Go To Folder dialog box to see the path names to the folders you've most recently Gone To. This is a handy way to get back to a folder you were looking in a few minutes ago.

One of your most basic skills in Windows is being able to select files, copy them, and move them.

To select an item (an icon or an item in a list), just click on it. To select more than one item, press Ctrl and click on each one. If they're next to each other, you can press Shift, click on the first one, and then click on the last one. Sometimes that's faster than Ctrl-clicking. Pressing Ctrl+A selects all the files in a window or list.

Selecting, Copying, and Moving

Selecting

▶ **Tip:** *If you want all but one or two items, select them all with Ctrl+A and then Ctrl-click on the few you don't want.*

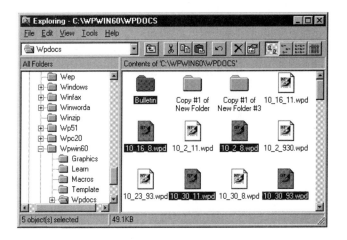

Ctrl-click to select several items

You can also select items by dragging over them. Click at the top-left corner of the group; then drag to the bottom-right corner. This trick works most elegantly on icons; you can do it in lists, but you're most likely to drag the first item instead. It also works best when you're selecting items in a rectangular area, but you can always go back and deselect the items you don't want.

Deselecting

You've selected stuff and you realize that you've got some things you didn't intend. Here's the secret of deselecting:

- To deselect one file, Ctrl-click on it.
- To deselect all but one file, click on that file.
- To deselect everything, click somewhere else.

Ctrl+Z, the Undo wiZard, deselects what you selected, too.

Copying and Moving

You can copy and move files and folders in My Computer or the Explorer by dragging and dropping them, or you can cut, copy, and paste them. This second method is new in Windows 95. You may find it easier to use until you get used to navigating to your folders, which can get a little convoluted. (See the section called "Looking into Windows" at the end of this chapter for some tricks you can use.) We'll cover the old way first.

Dragging

To move a file from one folder to another, just drag it to the new folder. If you want to copy an item from one folder to another on the same drive, press Ctrl as you drag; otherwise the item gets moved instead of copied.

- To copy a file to another drive, drag it.
- To move a file to another drive, Ctrl-drag it.
- To copy a file to another folder, same drive, Ctrl-drag it.
- To move a file to another folder, same drive, drag it.

It sounds easy, but in practice it's hard to find the folder you want to put the file in and keep the file selected at the same time. Try these techniques:

- In the Explorer, select the items you want to move or copy. Then scroll through the folders in the left pane until you find the one you want, while keeping the item selected in the pane on the right.

- Open multiple copies of the Explorer by double-clicking on it several times. Or select folders in the right-hand pane (Ctrl-click on them) and then Ctrl-double-click on the last one. These are both ways to have several different Explorer windows open on your desktop so you can copy and move files among them.

- Move folders by dragging them in the Explorer's left pane. Move files by dragging them *to* the folders in the Explorer's left pane.

- Navigate to other different folders quickly by using the drop-down list in the Explorer's toolbar.

Or try copying, cutting, and pasting instead of dragging.

Cutting, Copying, and Pasting

You can also select an item and press Ctrl+C to copy it or Ctrl+X to cut (move) it. Then go to the other drive or folder and press Ctrl+V (Paste) to put it there.

Some folks like the right-mouse-click technique, too. Or right-click on an item and choose Copy or Cut. Go to where you want it, right-click, and choose Paste..

And other folks like clicking on the Cut, Copy, and Paste icons on the toolbar. Go for whatever works.

Rewriting the Screen

This can drive you nuts if you aren't aware of it! If you copy or move something into another folder or switch floppy disks in a drive, the Explorer (or My Computer) doesn't automatically update the listing that you see on the screen. The item you copied or moved appears at the end of the window, and sometimes you can't see it! Press F5 to rewrite the screen so that it's up to date.

Renaming Files and Folders

Where's the menu with "Rename" on it? Well, there is one, but you don't have to use it. Just click on a file's name, and a box appears around it You may have to move the mouse just a little to get the box to appear, and be careful not to double-click, or you may open the file. Then type the new name and press Enter, or click with the mouse somewhere else.

▶ **Tip:** *You can press F2 to rename, too.*

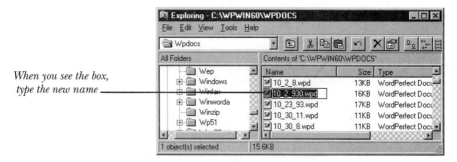

When you see the box,
type the new name

Creating a New Folder

To create a new folder, right-click in a My Computer or Explorer window and choose New; then choose Folder.

To create a new *file*, you have to use a program, such as WordPad or Lotus 1-2-3 or WordPerfect, depending on whether you're creating a spreadsheet or whatever.

Deleting Files and Folders

▶ **Tip:** *In Windows 95, nothing's really deleted (usually) until you empty the Recycle Bin.*

There's a Delete command on the Explorer's File menu. There's a Delete command on My Computer's File menu. A Delete command also appears if you right-click on an object. There's also a Delete key. It's easy to find. Use it.

To delete a file folder, select it and press Del. You'll be asked if you want to delete that folder—and all of its contents. Click Yes, and the folder and whatever's in it goes to the Recycle Bin.

The Recycle Bin

▶ **Tip:** *To bypass the Recycle Bin and really delete something, press Shift+Del. Be careful, because it's no easy feat to get it back.*

The Recycle Bin holds all the things you've deleted, until you empty it by choosing Empty Recycle Bin from its File menu. You can also right-click on the Recycle Bin's icon and choose Empty Recycle Bin, but it's safer to open it and see what's in it first.

The Recycle Bin *doesn't* hold things you delete from within your programs or from DOS, just stuff you delete at the desktop.

If you open a lot of windows on your desktop, it can get

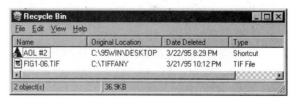

cluttered in a hurry. But you'll often want to be able to see into several windows at once if you're moving and copying things between folders. The trick here, if you recall it from Chapter 3, is to use the taskbar. Right-click on a blank spot on it; then choose Cascade or Tile Horizontally or Tile Vertically to arrange the open windows.

You can use a different technique to open several folders at once in the Explorer, which, as you recall, normally opens only one window at a time. Select a folder by right-clicking on it in the right pane; then choose Open. You can open any number of folders this way to see into all of them at once. You can drag to rearrange the windows if you need to see more of their contents, or right-click on the taskbar and choose Cascade, Tile Horizontally, or Tile Vertically.

Looking into Windows

▶ **Tip:** *In My Computer, Ctrl-double-click on a folder to open another window if you've chosen single browse mode.*

The Explorer and My Computer also let you do routine disk maintenance, such as formatting disks, copying files onto floppy disks, and making duplicates of floppy disks.

Copying files to floppies can get convoluted. Say that you want to copy an item from a folder on drive C to a floppy in drive A by using the Explorer. Click in the left pane to open the folder on drive C ; double-click on the folder you want in the right pane, click on the item you want to copy. Then use the scroll bars to display drive A listed under My Computer in the left-hand pane of the Explorer. Now all you have to do is drag that item's icon to the icon of drive A. That's one way.

Disk Work

Copying Files to Floppies

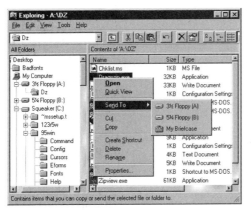

▶ **Tip:** *For a quick way to copy a file to a floppy disk, right-click on its name and choose Send To and your floppy drive.*

There's another way you might find easier: Put short-cuts to your floppy drives on the desktop. Do this now:

- Click in the Explorer's left pane and press Home, or open My Computer. You'll see your floppy drives listed.
- Drag them to the desktop. Click Yes when you're asked if you want to make a shortcut.

Now you can simply drag files to those shortcuts to copy them onto floppy disks. (Put a disk in the drive first, of course.)

Formatting Disks

If you need to format a floppy disk, put it in your disk drive. Then locate the icon for that floppy drive. If you've put a shortcut to it on the desktop, great. Just right-click on that shortcut. Without a shortcut, open My Computer or the Explorer. (Your drives are at the top of the list in the Explorer's left-hand pane.) Right-click on the disk drive's icon and choose Format.

Click the Quick button for a quick format that erases a used disk so you can use it again.

Copying Disks

Sometimes you'll want to make a duplicate copy of a floppy disk so that you can give it to somebody else or store it for safekeeping. To make a duplicate of a floppy disk, right-click on the icon of the floppy disk drive you want to use and choose Copy Disk.

Here's How

To	Do
See what's on your computer	Go to My Computer or the Explorer.
Go to My Computer	Double-click its icon on your desktop.
Go to the Explorer	Right-click on the Start button and choose Explore.
Look at the contents of a folder	Click on a folder in the Explorer's left pane, or double-click on a folder in My Computer.
View toolbars and status bars	Choose Toolbar and Status bar from the View menu in My Computer or the Explorer.
View file details	Click the Details icon on the toolbar in My Computer or the Explorer.
View file details that are often necessary	Choose Options from the View menu and *uncheck* the Hide MS-DOS files extensions box. *Check* the Display full MS-DOS path in the title bar. Click OK.
See the files you worked with most recently	Click on the Modified button when you're viewing details.
View files before folders	Click the Name button when you're viewing details.
Change the size of Explorer panes	Drag the bar between the two windows.
See the structure of your computer at a glance	Click on the down arrow next to whatever's listed at the top of the left-hand pane in My Computer and the Explorer.
Go to another folder	Click on it.

To	Do
See folders that are inside a folder	Click on the + next to a folder in the Explorer's left pane, or double-click on a folder in the right pane. In My Computer, double-click on a folder.
Open or close a folder in the Explorer's left pane	Click on it, or press the + and - keys on the numeric keypad when the folder's selected.
Go to the top of a My Computer/Explorer list or window	Press Home.
Go to the bottom of a My Computer/Explorer list or window	Press End.
Collapse the tree in the Explorer's left pane	Double-click on the Desktop icon at the beginning of the list of folders in the left-hand window. Or press the - on the numeric keypad.
Expand the tree in the Explorer's left pane	Double-click on the Desktop icon again, or select the drive and press the + on the numeric keypad.
Close a folder and all its containing folders	Shift-click on a folder window's Close button.
Go up one level in My Computer or the Explorer	Press Backspace.
Move folders to other locations	Drag them in the Explorer's left pane, or cut and paste.
Find a file or folder	Press F3 or choose Find from the Tools menu, choose Files or Folders, and enter a file or folder's name. Be sure the Look in box displays the name of your hard drive if you want to search the whole drive. Click Find Now.
Go to a folder	Choose Go To from the Explorer's Tools menu, type in the path to the folder or file you want to go to, and click OK.

To	Do
Go to a folder you went to	Click on the downward-pointing arrow next to the text box in the Go To Folder dialog box.
Select an item (an icon or an item in a list)	Click on it.
Select more than one item	Press Ctrl and click on each one.
Select adjacent items	Press Shift, click on the first one, and then click on the last one. Or drag over them: Click at the top-left corner of the group; then drag to the bottom- right corner.
Select all the files in a window or list	Press Ctrl+A.
Deselect one file	Ctrl-click on it.
Deselect all but one file	Click on that file.
Deselect everything	Click somewhere else, or press Ctrl+Z.
Copy a file to another drive	Drag or press Ctrl+C, Ctrl+V.
Move a file to another drive	Ctrl-drag or press Ctrl+X, Ctrl+V.
Copy a file to another folder on the same drive	Ctrl-drag or press Ctrl+C, Ctrl+V.
Move a file to another folder on the same drive	Drag or press Ctrl+X, Ctrl+V.
Open multiple folders in the Explorer	Ctrl-click on folders in the right-hand pane and then Ctrl-double-click on the last one, or open multiple copies of the Explorer by double-clicking on its icon.
Rename a file or folder	Click on its name and retype the new name. Or press F2.

To	Do
Create a new folder	Right-click in a My Computer or Explorer window and choose New; then choose Folder.
Delete an icon	Select it and press Del. It goes to the Recycle Bin.
Bypass the Recycle Bin	Press Shift+Del.
Empty the Recycle Bin	Choose Empty Recycle Bin from its File menu.
Arrange windows	Right-click on a blank spot on the taskbar; then choose Cascade or Tile Horizontally or Tile Vertically.
Create a shortcut to your floppy drives	Click in the Explorer's left pane and press Home, or open My Computer. Drag your floppy drive icons to the desktop.
Copy files onto a floppy disk	Drag them to the icon of the floppy disk drive, or right-click on them and choose Send To.
Format a floppy disk	Right-click on the icon of the floppy disk drive or its shortcut. Choose Format.
Erase a used disk	Right-click on the icon of the floppy disk drive or its shortcut. Choose Format. Click the Quick button.
Copy a floppy disk	Right-click on the icon of the floppy disk drive you want to use and choose Copy Disk.

Customizing Windows

The real secret to not getting overly frustrated with Windows 95 lies in setting it up to work the way you want it to. It's particularly important to get your desktop set up so that you can easily find things you use often. You wouldn't keep your ballpoint pen in the back of the bottom drawer in your filing cabinet, and neither should you leave the Windows programs and tools you use every day buried way down where Windows puts them.

Customizing Windows 95 has another side benefit: you get to do a lot of fun stuff, like changing screen colors and screen savers, while learning how to manipulate the interface at the same time. It's safe; it's not scary, and you see the results of your efforts right away.

This chapter tells you about some—but not all—ways you can customize Windows 95. As usual, if there's something I think you really ought to do, I'll say so. Otherwise all the custom-tailoring is up to you.

Setting up Your Desktop

Before you go any further, get your desktop set up so you can find things.

Shortcuts on the Desktop

Shortcuts are great, because you can stick them all over the place. Put shortcuts to the things you use when you start up and then return to several times a day right there on the desktop. How about:

- Your e-mail program?
- Your floppy drives?

- Your network drives, if you're on a network?

- Your letterhead or memo form?

- Your printer? (You'll see more about this in Chapter 7.)

- Your word processing program?

- Your spreadsheet program?

- The Calculator?

- The Phone Dialer? (This is so cool.)

- Your solitaire game?

Go to My Computer or the Explorer and locate those files, one by one. Then press Ctrl and drag each one to the desktop. Choose Create Shortcut here. It may help if you choose Options from the Views menu and uncheck the Hide MS-DOS file extensions button, because then you can identify program files by their .EXE extension.

▶ **Tip:** *Advanced trick: Look at the Start menu in the figure. See that Desktop folder? The Desktop is a hidden folder inside your Window folder, and putting it on the Start menu's a very clever thing to do, because you can get back to the desktop any time by pressing Ctrl+Esc. Use the Views/Options menu in My Computer/the Explorer to display hidden files.*

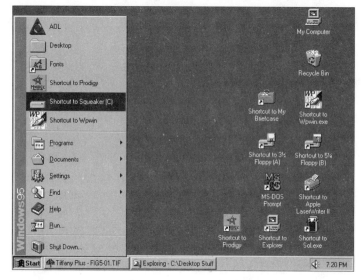

Your Start Menu

Put programs you use *often* and need to be able to start from within other programs on the Start menu. It's so easy! Just drag a program's icon to the Start menu button, and will appear on your Start menu, where it's very handy. It will be on the main Start menu, so you don't have to mouse over to Programs and then mouse to the program you want and then figure out exactly what it is that you want... You get the idea.

Consider the same candidates as in the list above. There's an additional benefit: Anything you put on the Start menu can be accessed any time you press Ctrl+Esc, which brings up the Start menu even when you're working inside another program. If you use anything often, it's a good candidate for either the desktop or the Start menu.

▶ **Tip:** *Make as many shortcuts as you need. If you need a shortcut to, say, the Calculator, in three different places, make three shortcuts of it and put them wherever you want them.*

Your Own Program Groups

You can create your own folders inside the Programs folder on the Start menu. Just drag shortcuts to the Programs folder inside the Start Menu folder. You might want to create a folder called Jones Project, say, and put in it shortcuts to all the letters and reports and spreadsheets you work with on that project. Or create one called Mary's Letters with shortcuts to all your personal correspondence with Mary. Or...

Your StartUp Folder

Put any programs you want to start up with every day in your StartUp folder. If you always start out the day getting on, say, America Online, start it along with Windows 95. Just drag a shortcut to it into your StartUp folder. This folder's in your Windows directory in the Start menu folder, and you'll need to go over to My Computer or the Explorer to find it.

Deleting and Renaming Shortcuts

There are a few shortcut "rules" you should be aware of. If you delete the original object, its shortcuts aren't deleted, so you can wind up with useless icons wherever you've put shortcuts. Be careful about deleting something you've made a lot of shortcuts to, or moving it to a different folder.

But feel free to go ahead and delete shortcuts. If you delete a shortcut, the original isn't deleted. You can delete one shortcut, though, and all the rest of the shortcuts to that item, if there are others, will stay intact.

If you rename the original, all its shortcuts aren't automatically renamed. But you can rename shortcuts. They don't have to match the original's name.

The Fun Stuff The things we just looked at are more or less essential. Now we'll get to the fun stuff.

Move the Taskbar Drag the taskbar to move it to the top or sides of the screen, wherever you want it. Some folks think it's easier to read on the right or left side of the screen. You can also drag its edge to make it bigger or smaller.

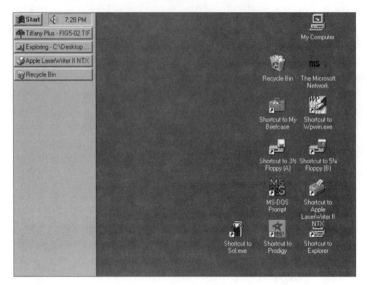

Right-click on the taskbar and choose Properties to change even more things. Clicking Auto-Hide makes the taskbar invisible until you drag the mouse over it. To make your Start menu smaller, click Show small icons in Start menu.

Double-click on My Computer. Right-click drive C or whatever your hard drive is. Choose Properties and click the General tab. Type a new label for your hard drive. (Squeaker is a cat, not a bad hard drive.)

Rename Your Computer

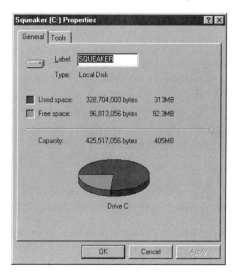

You can change a shortcut's icon. This is fun, too, and it gets you moving through your filing system. Right-click on a shortcut icon and choose Properties. Then click the Shortcut tab and the Change icon button.

Change Shortcut Icons

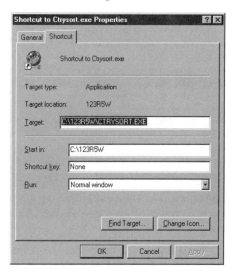

You'll see the Change Icon window. Click the Browse button and look for more icons. They crop up in the most unsuspecting places. Just keep looking until you find something interesting; then double-click on it to choose it for your shortcut. *Hint:* Go to your Windows 95 directory and look in Drvspace to see these.

Change the Desktop's Pattern and Wallpaper

Right-click on the desktop; then choose Properties from the pop-up menu. To change the background, click the Background tab. Pick a pattern, or pick wallpaper. If you choose wallpaper, keep Tile checked next to Display if you want an all-over wallpaper pattern to cover your desktop background. Clicking Center just produces one tiny wallpaper pattern in the middle of the screen.

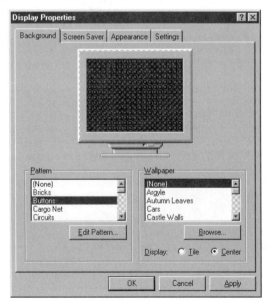

If you choose a pattern, you might also like to change the desktop's background color. Click the Appearance tab. Then click Color next to Desktop listed under Item and pick a new color. Click Apply to see the effects of what you chose! When you like it, click OK.

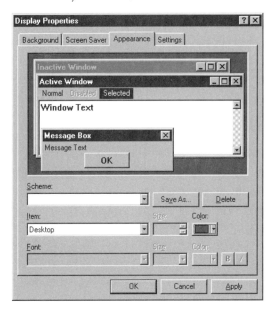

In the Background tab, click the Edit Pattern button, and you'll see the Pattern Editor, where you can click on each individual pixel of a pattern to create a custom pattern. When you get the pattern the way you like it, give it a new name and click Add and Done.

Create a Custom Pattern

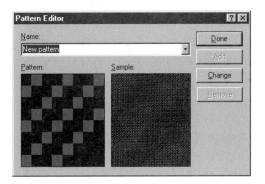

▶ **Tip:** *Be sure to give your pattern a new name, or it will replace the pattern you're editing.*

Change the Whole Color Scheme

Click the Appearance tab; then, under Scheme, click the downward-pointing arrow to see a list of preset schemes.

Too bad this book isn't in color. The one below is High Contrast White (large), which is good if you have a laptop or if you have trouble reading the screen. Other color scheme opinions: Lilac and Rainy Day are for the Addams Family. Avoid Wheat at all costs. Some are better than others.

▶ **Tip:** *Don't choose the same color for Menu and Font, or you won't be able to read the text in your menus!*

Create Your Own Color Scheme

If you don't like any of the preset schemes, with a little patience, you can create your own. Pick a color scheme that's fairly similar to what you want, so that you can just edit it instead of doing everything from scratch. Then click on the item you want to change in the sample screen—say, Active Title Bar. Click in the Color box for that item. Click Other to mix a custom color. Here are a few personal tips for choosing colors. Keep the type that you'll be reading in a dark color, preferably black or dark blue. Keep the window background a very light tint, to keep it easy on your eyes for long stretches of time. Try a light green, light blue, light yellow, or white.

If you want an easy-on-the-eyes light background, mix your own very pale shade (see below). Also keep the active title bar and the menu bar in a dark or strong color, so that you can read the words on them! The scroll bars and other places where you don't have to read? Go wild. Use magenta if you like, or any of the neon colors.

When the color scheme looks good (click Apply to see it on the whole desktop), click Save As and give the scheme a name so you can use it again. Give it a name that's different from the one it already has, so that you can tell which scheme's yours and which came with Windows.

If you create a lot of color schemes and later decide that some of them are really ugly, you can delete them with the Delete button on the Appearance tab.

You can "mix" 16 more custom colors and use them in your color schemes! To mix your own colors, click in the Color box and then click Other at the bottom of the color palette. You may have to move the window up a bit to see it. You'll see the Color selector, where you can move the color refiner cursor (the little array of dots) to put a color in the Color/Solid box. Wow! This book doesn't do it justice. The color box is an array of hues from orange to yellow to blue to purple to red, going from left to right.

Mix Your Own Colors

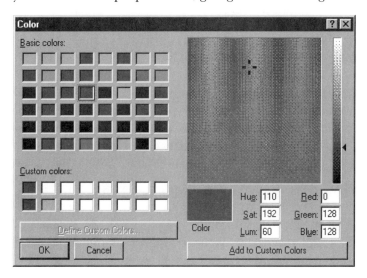

On this multicolored part of the screen, you'll see a small black "box"—four little black dots. That's the color refiner cursor. To change colors, click on a color under Basic colors that's close to the shade you want. Drag the color refiner cursor until a color you like appears in the Color box.

Once you've got the color you want, you can make it brighter or darker (adjust its luminosity) by dragging in the vertical luminosity bar. You can also adjust a color by changing the values next to Hue (to change the color), Sat (to change the saturation, or purity of color), and Lum (to change the color's luminosity, or brightness).

To increase the amount of red, green, or blue in a color, change the values in the Red, Green, and Blue boxes.

As you change colors, you'll see the new color in the Color box. When you've got a color the way you want it click Add to Custom Colors to add your new color to the palette. When you're done, click OK. From then on, you can use that new color in your color schemes.

Change the Screen Font

Back at the Appearance tab, you can change the font that's used on the screen. If you want a different (probably larger) font for the text on the screen, choose the screen item you want to change from the pop-up list under Item (Menu, Message Box, Icon Title, Active Title Bar, Inactive Title Bar, etc.). Click the downward-pointing arrow under Font; then choose a different font and size.

▶ **Tip:** *Avoid script fonts, Courier, and anything truly weird like OzHandicraft.*

Choose a Screen Saver

Click the Screen Saver tab to pick a screen saver. (Right-click on the desktop and choose Properties if you're not already there.) Click the downward-pointing arrow under Screen Saver to see a list of the screen savers that come with Windows 95. There's a sample on the next page.

▶ **Tip:** *Click the Settings button to see what else you can change about a screen saver's appearance.*

Set a Wait time to change the number of minutes that pass before the screen saver comes on after you last use the keyboard or mouse. You'll see a sample of the screen saver in action on the miniature screen; click Preview to see it full-screen size. Move the mouse slightly to get back to the Screen Saver tab. Click OK to set your choice.

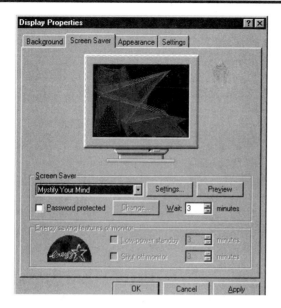

Hidden all over Windows 95 are settings you can custom-tailor to suit yourself. Here are a few of the most common ones you might want to change.

More Neat Things You Can Change

If you get tired of the Windows sounds, turn the sound volume down or off. Click on the little speaker icon next to the time on the taskbar. You'll see a Mute box and a slider volume control. Check the Mute box to turn the sound completely off, or drag the slider down to decrease the volume.

Turn off the Sound

Choose Settings from the Start menu and click Control Panel. Double-click on the Sounds icon. You'll see a list of "events," such as Start Windows and Exit Windows.

   The preset event sounds get boring after a while, so get a collection of sounds (.WAV files) and get creative. They're available on disk, on CD-ROMs, and from online services, or you can use the Sound Recorder accessory to record your own sounds, if you have a sound card and a microphone.

   Once you get some new sound files on your hard disk, double-click on the Sounds icon in the Control Panel folder and click on the event whose sound you want to change. Click Browse and locate the sound you want to

Change the System Sounds

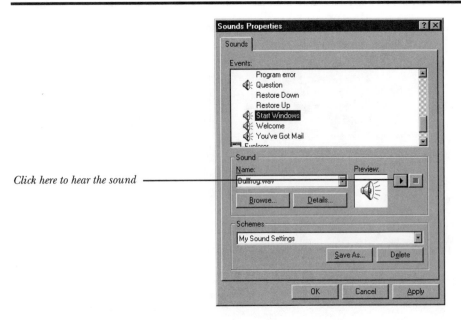

Click here to hear the sound —————

use. Click the right-pointing arrow next to Preview to hear a sample of the sound. Double-click on the sound's name to choose that sound for the event you selected.

You can save different sound schemes by clicking the Save As button.

▶ **Tip:** *Click the Details icon so you can pick short (small) sounds for things like Asterisk, Critical Stop, Exclamation, and so forth—the beep stuff. You don't want a 5-second sound every time Windows beeps.*

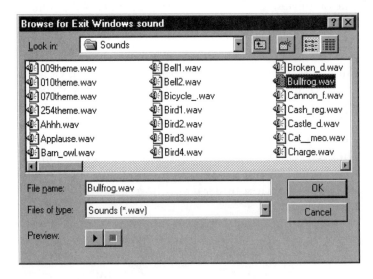

Don't like the "feel" of the mouse? Go to the Control Panel folder and double-click the Mouse icon. Click the Buttons tab to change the mouse from Right-handed to Left-handed, which reverses the actions of the right and left mouse buttons. Click the Buttons tab to set the double-click speed.

Set Up Your Mouse

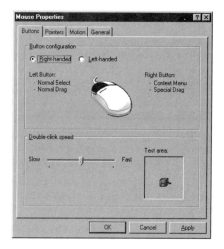

▶ **Tip:** *To tell that you've got the double-click speed set right, double-click in the Test area until the jack pops up out of the box.*

Click the Pointers tab if you have trouble seeing the mouse pointer on the screen. Click the downward-pointing arrow under Scheme and pick a larger set of pointers, or change individual pointers by choosing each one and browsing for a different cursor file. To start, look in your System folder inside your Windows folder.

Click the Motion tab to speed up the mouse pointer or slow it down. If you have a laptop, click Show pointer trails so you can locate the pointer more easily on the screen.

Customize the Key Repeat Rate

▶ Tip: *If you're having trouble locating the insertion point, speed up the cursor blink rate by dragging its slider bar to the right.*

To change the rate a key repeats when you hold it down, double-click on the Keyboard icon in the Control Panel folder. Move the Repeat rate slider bar. You may prefer a light touch or a heavy one. Use the Repeat delay slider bar to set how long you want Windows 95 to wait before it recognizes that you're holding down a key so it will repeat. Test your choices in the test box. Click OK to set your choices.

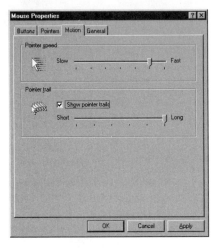

Change the Date and Time Formats

Go to the Control Panel folder and click the Time and the Date tabs to change the style of the date and time. To change the date and time themselves, just double-click on the time on the taskbar!

Make the Help Text Bigger

Can't read a Help topic? Right-click inside a Help topic; then choose Font. Finally, pick Large.

Keep Help on Top

While you're learning something new, it's often helpful to keep Help on Top. This means that if you click outside the Help window to try something out, the Help topic will stay displayed on your screen. When you're looking at a Help topic, click its Options button and choose Keep Help on Top from the Help window's Options menu; then click On Top. Now the Help topic will stay visible as you test out what it says.

Here's How

To	Do
Create a shortcut	Drag a program's icon (or Ctrl-drag anything else) to the desktop. Choose Create Shortcut here.
Put something on the Start menu	Drag its icon to the Start menu button.
Bring up the Start menu	Press Ctrl+Esc.
Start a program automatically	Put a shortcut to it in your Startup folder (in your Windows directory in the Start menu folder).
Move the taskbar	Drag it.
Change the taskbar's properties	Right-click on the taskbar and choose Properties.
Name your computer	Double-click My Computer. Right-click drive C or whatever your hard drive is. Choose Properties and click the General tab. Type a new label for your hard drive.
Change a shortcut's icons	Right-click on a shortcut icon and choose Properties. Then click the Shortcut tab and the Change icon button.
Change the desktop's pattern and wallpaper	Right-click on the desktop; then choose Properties from the pop-up menu that appears. Click the Background tab.
Change the desktop pattern's color	Right-click on the desktop; then choose Properties from the pop-up menu that appears. Click the desktop property sheet's Appearance tab.
Create a custom pattern	Right-click on the desktop; then choose Properties from the pop-up menu that appears. In the desktop property sheet's Background tab, click the Edit Pattern button.

To	Do
Change the whole color scheme	Right-click on the desktop; then choose Properties from the pop-up menu that appears. Click the desktop property sheet's Appearance tab; then, under Scheme, click the downward-pointing arrow to see a list of preset schemes.
Mix your own colors	Right-click on the desktop; then choose Properties from the pop-up menu that appears. In the desktop property sheet's Appearance tab, click in the Color box and then click Other at the bottom of the color palette.
Change the screen font	Right-click on the desktop; then choose Properties from the pop-up menu that appears. In the desktop property sheet's Appearance tab, pick a different font.
Choose a screen saver	Right-click on the desktop; then choose Properties from the pop-up menu that appears. Click the desktop property sheet's Screen Saver tab.
Turn off the sound	Click on the little speaker icon next to the time on the taskbar.
Change the system sounds	Choose Settings from the Start menu and click Control Panel. Double-click on the Sounds icon.
Set up your mouse	Choose Settings from the Start menu and click Control Panel. Double-click on the Mouse icon.
Change the mouse from right-handed to left-handed	Choose Settings from the Start menu and click Control Panel. Double-click on the Mouse icon. Click the Buttons tab.
Change the pointer's speed	Choose Settings from the Start menu and click Control Panel. Double-click on the Mouse icon. Click the Motion tab.
Customize the key repeat rate	Double-click on the Keyboard icon in the Control Panels folder. Move the Repeat rate slider bar.
Change the date and time formats	Double-click on the Control Panels folder's Regional Settings icon and click the Time and the Date tabs.

To	Do
Change the date and time	Double-click on the time on the taskbar.
Make the Help text bigger	Right-click inside a Help topic; then choose Font.
Keep Help on top	When you're looking at a Help topic, click its Options button and choose Keep Help on Top; then click On Top.

Working with Programs

Once you've learned the basics of how to work in one program's window, you've learned the basics of how to work in just about any program's window. And all Windows programs have many other things in common, in addition to how you work with their windows. You can start them all the same way, and once you're in them, you'll find similar menus in them. So in this chapter, we'll look at the basic techniques for starting programs, switching between them, copying and pasting among them, and shutting them down.

Not surprisingly, since Windows 95 is designed to run several programs at once, it gives you many different ways to start programs. Here are all the ones I can think of (surely there are more). You can open a program:

Starting Programs

- From the Start menu or shortcuts on the Start menu
- From My Computer
- From the Explorer
- From its icon on the desktop
- From the Find dialog box
- From a DOS window
- From the Documents folder
- From the Run command
- By dragging and dropping

- By right-clicking on a document icon

- By sending a document to a program

We'll look at all these different techniques. You can mix and match as the occasion suits you.

From the Start Menu

Tip: *Press Ctrl+Esc to display the Start menu.*

When Windows 95 is installed, it searches your hard disk and puts all the programs it finds there in a folder named Programs on the Start menu. If the program you want to run is listed there, just click on the Start menu, click on Programs, and then click on the folder with the program you want to open. Click on the program's name to start it.

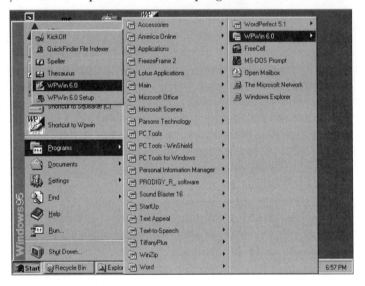

▶ **Tip:** *Right-click on the Start button and choose Open to see the shortcuts on your Start menu.*

That's a lot of mousing—sometimes precision mousing—because there are several cascading menus to choose from. There are better, faster ways to open programs, but you may not know about them at first.

From Shortcuts on the Start Menu

You can put shortcuts to programs you use frequently at the top level of the Start menu so you don't have to mouse so far to see them. Just drag the program's icon to the Start button. That's all you have to do, and it will appear as a shortcut on the Start menu, where you can click on it to start the program.

If there are folders you use often, put them as short-cuts on your Start menu, too.

The Start menu can only hold so many items, and then it fills up. To have access to everything stored on your hard drive, floppy drives, CD-ROM, and network drives, use My Computer. It's right there on your desktop, easy to find.

Double-click on the My Computer icon on your desktop. Then double-click on your hard drive icon. Double-click on the folder that has the program you want to open in it. Finally, double-click on the icon of the program you want to run.

See Chapter 4 for lots of different techniques for using My Computer and finding your way around in there.

The Explorer is more versatile than My Computer, because it shows the hierarchy of your filing system at a glance, and you can copy and move files and folders by using its two window panes. To go to the Explorer, right-click on the Start button and choose Explore.

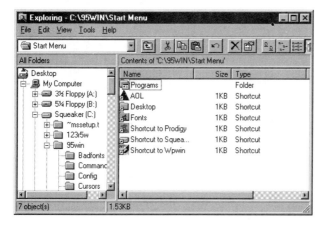

From My Computer

From the Explorer

Click on a folder in the left-hand pane of the Explorer window to open that folder. You'll see the folder's contents in the right pane as you open folders. When you locate the program you want to run, double-click on it.

See Chapter 4 for lots of different techniques for using the Explorer and finding your way around in there.

From Its Icon on the Desktop

If you've had the foresight to put programs you use most often on your desktop by making shortcuts to them, you can simply double-click on a program's icon on the desktop to start it.

From the Find Utility

Once you've found a program with the Find utility (F3), you can start it from there, without hunting for its real location. Just double-click on the program or document's name in the list of found files.

From the Documents Folder

The Documents folder on the Start menu lists the last 15 programs or documents you've opened lately from the desktop. It "remembers" from session to session, too. You can click on one of these programs or documents to open them again.

With the Run Command

If you remember the path to a program or folder (all the folders it's in), you can choose Run from the Start menu and type that path in the Open box and click OK.

▶ **Tip:** *Ctrl+Esc r brings up the Run command if you're working in a program.*

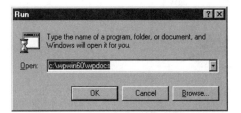

If you don't recall the path name, click the Browse button. The window you see automatically displays only program files, so it's relatively easy to open the folder you want to look in and locate the program you want to run. When you find it, double-click on its icon to start it.

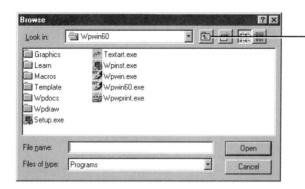

Click here or press Backspace to go up one level when you're browsing.

For more on path names, what they are, and why you can't get away from them, see Chapter 4.

From a DOS Window

For you DOS folks, you can even start Windows programs from DOS! If you're at the command line, typing the command that normally starts the program will open it. Of course, you'll have to remember its path name, so in practice that means entering something complicated like **c:\123r5w\123** (this one's for Lotus 1-2-3 release 4 for Windows) or whatever the path to the program is.

There's also a new DOS Start command, as in **start c:\123r5w\123**. You don't have to use the word "start," but you can if you want to.

By Dragging and Dropping

Windows 95 gives you several ways to start programs by dragging and dropping:

- Drag a document's icon to a program's icon to open it.

- Drag a document's icon to a program's shortcut to open it.

- Drag a document's icon to an open program window to open it.

The catch is that the program must "know" about that document. If it's a document that the program originally created, dragging and dropping works fine. If the document was created by another program, the program you drop it on may try to open it, but you'll see garbage on the screen, which you may if you try to open a WordPerfect document in WordPad.

▶ **Tip:** *You can use My Computer or the Explorer to tell Windows 95 what "type" a document is if it keeps telling you it doesn't know. Choose Options from the Views menu and click the File Types tab.*

By Right-Clicking on a Document Icon

If you right-click on a document's icon, you'll get a pop-up menu starting with Open With... Choose that, and you can specify the program you want to open the document with.

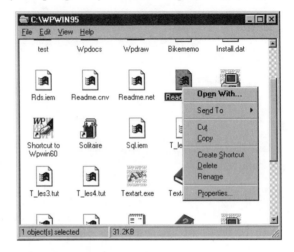

By Sending a Document to a Program

This one's a little advanced, but it's not so bad. If you right-click on a document icon, you'll also see a Send To command. You can add programs to the list of Send to choices. Here's how to do that.

First, in the Explorer, make all your files visible. Choose Options from the View menu, click the View tab, and click Show all files. Now click OK, and you'll be able to see all your files and folders. You need to do this to make the Send To folder visible.

Now locate the program you want to be able to open files with and drag (or Ctrl-drag if you're dragging a shortcut) to the desktop to create a shortcut to it. Then locate the Send To folder (it's in your Windows 95 folder) and drag the program's shortcut to that folder.

Now try right-clicking on a document and choosing Send To. In addition to your floppy drives, you'll see the program you just created a shortcut for listed.

Starting up with a Program

This one's not advanced at all. Any program you put in a folder named StartUp in your Windows\Start Menu folder directory will automatically start when you start Windows. You might want to start up with your word processing program. Or America Online, or your Internet provider.

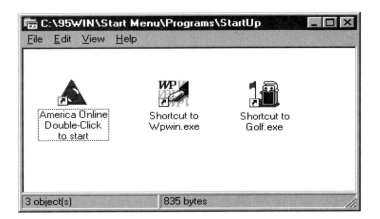

Drag shortcuts to the StartUp folder to have them start when Windows starts.

Exiting from Programs

For a fast exit from a program, double-click on the System menu icon in the program window's upper-left corner. Or press Alt+F4. Either way, you'll be asked to save any unsaved work. You can also choose Exit from a program's File menu, or click the Close box in the upper-right corner of the program window.

Or use this neat trick: Right-click on the program's button on the taskbar and choose Close. You'll get a chance to save any documents that haven't been saved.

Switching Between Programs

The taskbar displays the names of open programs and folders, so clicking on an item's name on the taskbar is usually the fastest way to switch between the programs you've got running. But there are other ways to switch between programs, too.

Fast Alt+Tab Switching

Press Alt and hold it down. Then press Tab repeatedly. You'll see the names of the programs, windows, and folders you have running on the screen, one by one. A box appears around the one that will become active if you let go of the Alt key. When you see the name of the program you want to switch to, release the Alt key.

Alt+Esc Cycling   If you press Alt+Esc repeatedly instead of Alt+Tab, you'll actually cycle through all the open windows on your desktop and highlight the minimized windows that are listed on the taskbar. I like Alt+Tab better.

Can't See the Taskbar?   If the taskbar gets covered up and you can't see it, you may have turned on Auto Hide. Move the mouse pointer to the very bottom of the screen, or to the side of the window where you usually display the taskbar. The taskbar should appear.

If you *still* can't find the taskbar, double-click in the window's title bar. That should shrink the window so you can see the taskbar.

Need to Get to the Desktop?   You may sometimes need to get back to the desktop instead of just finding the taskbar, but your screen is all covered up with windows! There's a trick you can use to clean off your screen quickly: Right-click on a blank area of the taskbar and choose Minimize All Windows. To get the windows back the way they were, do the same thing and choose Undo Minimize All.

Doing the "New" Windows   The new Windows 95 interface is visible in all the programs you run, even those that weren't specifically designed for Windows 95. So even familiar programs may take a bit of getting used to again. For example, the Close box is at the top-*right* corner of the window now. The Windows taskbar appears at the bottom of the screen. This window's from WordPad, which comes with Windows 95 as an accessory.

In addition, you'll see new Open and Save As dialog boxes in Windows 95 programs. These are mini-File Managers themselves. We'll look at them first.

Open Dialog Boxes   You'll see some of the same icons in Open and Save As dialog boxes that you see in Explorer and My Computer windows. Notice there's a new icon that lets you create a new folder right there in the dialog box. (Not all of the new dialog boxes will look exactly like the one on the next page, but the basics are the same.)

▶ **Tip:** *Most of these factoids apply to Save As dialog boxes, too.*

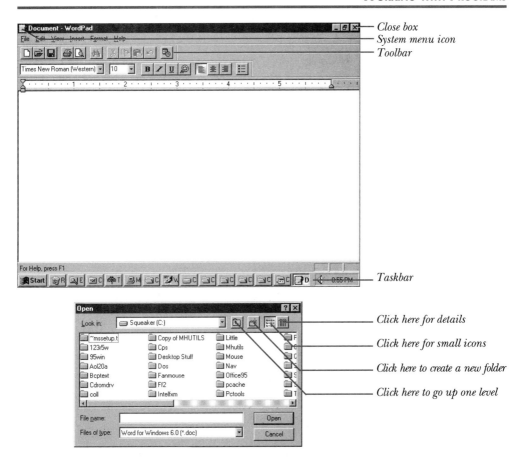

Close box
System menu icon
Toolbar

Taskbar

Click here for details

Click here for small icons

Click here to create a new folder

Click here to go up one level

Double-click on folders to open them and move through your filing system

Click the down arrow next to the Look in box to see a My Computer-style list, where you can examine the contents of other drives and the folders on them.

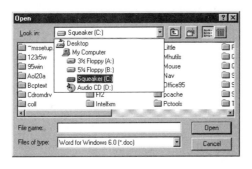

▶ **Tip:** *To open a document after you've started a program, choose Open from its File menu or click the "open folder" icon on the toolbar. To save a document, press Ctrl+S, choose Save from the File menu, or click the little disk icon on the toolbar. The first time you save a document, you'll see the Save As dialog box.*

As you select a file in the list, its name appears in the File name box. Press Enter or click Open to open it. An even faster way to open a document is to double-click on it in the list.

Viewing Details

If you view file details by clicking on the far-right icon on the toolbar, you can sort the files in the list. Just as in My Computer or Explorer windows, click on a column heading in an Open or Save As dialog to sort the contents of that column. Click on Modified to see the most recent files first.

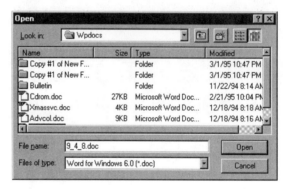

Navigating Lists

You may need to scroll to see all of a list. If you do, you'll see scroll bars at the bottom, or side, or bottom of the dialog box. Instead of scrolling, if you know the character the file you're looking for begins with, type it, and you'll go directly to that part of the list.

Pressing Home takes you to the beginning of a list, and pressing End takes you to the end. These are handy keyboard shortcuts for long lists.

▶ **Tip:** *Press PgUp and PgDn to move through a list, too.*

Renaming files

You can even rename documents and folders in an Open or Save As dialog box. Click on the name, or select it and press F2. Type the new name and press Enter. Pressing Ctrl+Z will undo the renaming if you haven't done anything else.

Using Wildcards

These new-style Open dialog boxes even have an advantage over My Computer and the Explorer. You can use wildcards in the File name box to see names of files that match a certain pattern, such as A*.* to see all files beginning with A in a folder. (This works only on files, not folders.)

Here's how that goes. The wildcard character * stands for any number of characters, or none at all, and ? stands for one character or none at all. For example, if you have several files beginning with C (as Calc, Calendar, Codes, and so forth), entering c* in the File name box will display just those file names. This is convenient for displaying only the documents you're interested in.

▶ **Tip:** *If you don't see what you're looking for, try clicking on the down arrow next to Files of type and choosing All Files (*.*)*

If the program you're working in lets you open more than one window at a time, you can Ctrl-click on the documents you want to open in the Open dialog box and then double-click on the last one to open them all. (WordPad won't let you do this, but other word processing programs, like Word and WordPerfect, will.)

Opening Several Documents

You can copy and move documents (and folders, too) from one folder to another by using these Open and Save As dialogs. Highlight an item and press Ctrl+C for Copy or Ctrl+X for Cut (which is the same as Move). Then open the folder you want to put what you've cut or copied in and press Ctrl+V for Paste.

Right-clicking on an item and choosing Cut or Copy works, too. And so does dragging and dropping. Just drag an item to move it, or press Ctrl and drag it to copy it. You'll see a tiny plus sign when you're copying.

If you can't see the folder you want to put the item in, there's a way around that. Make the program window less than full-screen size before you choose Open or Save As, so that you can see part of the desktop. Now drag to move (or Ctrl-drag to copy) the icon of the document you want to the desktop, open another folder in the dialog box, and drag the icon back from the desktop to put it in the folder.

Moving and Copying Documents

These new Open and Save as dialog boxes even let you create shortcuts. Right-click on the item and choose Create Shortcut. The shortcut appears at the end of the list, where you can drag it to the desktop or the Start menu, where it'll be more useful.

Creating Shortcuts

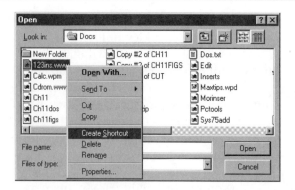

> ▶ **Tip:** *Items you delete from programs that weren't designed especially for Windows 95 won't go to the Recycle Bin!*

Deleting Files

Yes, you can delete in Open and Save as dialog boxes, too. Select a file (or files, if you can) and press Del, or right-click and choose Delete.

Printing

You don't even have to open a document to print it any more. Right-click on its name in an Open dialog box; then choose Print. This won't work for folders, or if Windows 95 doesn't know what kind of document you've selected.

Sneak Peeks

Right-click on a file in an Open or Save As dialog box; then choose QuickView to see what's in it. You'll be taken to a QuickView window, where you can open the file by clicking on the far-left icon, make the font larger or smaller by clicking the two icons with an A on them, or choose Page View from the View menu to see the document page by page. A really handy feature.

> ▶ **Tip:** *You can do this in My Computer and the Explorer, too!*

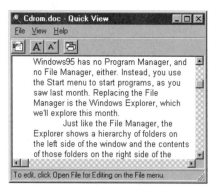

The Find command is also available in Open and Save As dialog boxes, if you know where to look. Right-click on a folder; then choose Find to locate the file or folder you're hunting for. You'll be taken directly to the Find utility.

Find Things, Too

You can even go directly to the Explorer from an Open or Save As dialog box, to use its split-pane view that lets you see your filing system. Right-click on a folder (not the one that's in the Look in box) and choose Explore.

Going to the Explorer

Save As dialog boxes are pretty similar to Open dialog boxes. Basically, you open the folder you want to save the document in (in the Save in box) and then type a name that you want the document to have (in the File name box). These dialog boxes also have a Save as Type drop-down list you can use to save a document as a different file type—as Text Only or Rich Text Format, for example (this lets you open it in almost any word processing program).

Save As Dialog Boxes

In addition, you can use a Save As dialog box to do something you *can't* do in the Explorer or My Computer: rename and copy files at the same time.

If you want to make a copy of a file under a different name or in a different location, or both, enter a different name for the file in the Save as text box. If you want the document to be saved in a different folder, open the Save in list and double-click on the folder you want it saved in.

▶ **Tip:** *Use Save As to copy and rename files at the same time.*

Cutting, Copying, and Pasting between Programs

One of the big reasons people use Windows is that it lets them copy and move text and graphics between programs by cutting, copying, and pasting. This saves a lot of time, because you can copy something in one program and paste in it another program without having to type it again, or draw it again, or calculate it again, or whatever.

You've seen those Copy, Cut, and Paste commands and their keyboard equivalents Ctrl+C, Ctrl+X, and Ctrl+V, because you can use them at the Windows desktop and in My Computer and the Explorer and in all those Open and Save as dialog boxes, too. You can also use them in your programs.

You'll also see Cut, Copy, and Paste commands on the Edit menus in your programs. As their names imply, you use them just as you would use scissors and glue to cut and paste material you've selected in the program you're working with. You can also use them to copy and paste between programs.

> **Tip:** *What you delete (with Del or Backspace) doesn't go to the Clipboard. You can usually get it back with Undelete or Undo in your Windows programs.*

Whatever you copy or cut with these commands *in your programs* goes to a special holding place called the Clipboard. Whatever's on the Clipboard doesn't go away until you copy or cut something else. You can paste it over and over again in just about any document.

Copying

> **Tip:** *To copy text that takes up more than one screen, click at the beginning of what you want to copy; then press Shift and scroll to the end of what you want to copy and click again.*

To copy text (or graphics), select it and press Ctrl+C. You can also right-click on it and choose Copy, or choose Copy from the program's Edit menu, or click the Copy icon on the program's toolbar (this icon can look two tiny documents, or a tiny clipboard; it varies from program to program). Ctrl+C's easy to remember, and fast.

Once you've copied something, you can paste it over and over again until you copy or cut something else. The Clipboard holds one item at a time.

Cutting

> **Tip:** *Cutting's the same as moving. To move an item, cut it and paste it somewhere else.*

To cut (or move) something, select it and press Ctrl+X. This is another handy shortcut to memorize. You can also right-click on a selection and choose Cut, or choose Cut from the program's Edit menu, or click the Cut icon on the program's toolbar (this icon often looks like a pair of scissors).

Ctrl+V is the shortcut for Paste. To paste, put the cursor where you want the item you copied or cut to appear and press Ctrl+V. You can also right-click on a selection and choose Paste, or choose Paste from the program's Edit menu, or click the Paste icon on the program's toolbar (this icon often looks like a paste pot or a clipboard; it varies among programs).

Pasting

▶ **Tip:** *You won't be able to paste unless you've copied or cut something first.*

In many Windows programs, you can copy and move text and graphics by dragging and dropping the selection. Basically, drag over what you want to move and then put the cursor inside the selection. Press the left mouse button and drag to put it in another location. You'll see the mouse pointer change shape as you do this.

Dragging

OLE (pronounced oh-LAY) stands for Object Linking and Embedding, which is a very cool thing to do, although not all programs will let you do it.When you double-click on a lined or embedded object, you're taken back to the original program that created the object. So you could embed part of a spreadsheet in a word processing document, say, and then be able to go back to your spreadsheet program and edit the data directly from your document. Or you could link a graphic image from a drawing program and be able to open the drawing program to revise the image by double-clicking on it.

OLE!

What's the difference between linking and embedding? When you link an object (text, data, or graphics), you can double-click on it to start the program that originally created it, and the changes you make will take effect in all the other documents that object's linked to. When you embed an object, you can double-click on it to start the program that originally created it, and your changes take place only in that one document.

This stuff sounds a lot more advanced than it really is. Actually, in practice, it's pretty easy. You do this magic by using the Paste Link and Paste Special commands on your program's Edit menu. Starting out is always the same: Copy what you want to link or embed.

Linking

▶ **Tip:** *Shortcuts are actually links. You can drag shortcuts to programs and other documents into documents or mail messages, and you'll create an instant link.*

▶ **Tip:** *If you can't do OLE with a program, you won't see these commands.*

To create a link from one document to another:

- Select the information you want to link.
- Copy it.
- Go to the document where you want the information to appear and put the insertion point where you want it.
- Choose Paste Special from the program's Edit menu. (In some programs, you may see Paste Link right on the Edit menu.)
- Choose Paste Link and the format you want to use.

Now you can double-click on the linked object to return to its original program. If you change the data in the original file, it changes in all the documents it's linked to. Linking works best in projects that several people are working on and sending around for review and editing, or in several documents that contain information from one source.

Embedding

▶ **Tip:** *If you edit embedded data, it changes only in the document it's embedded in.*

Embedding puts the data in your file. When you select that data by double-clicking on it, you go to the program that created the embedded data. If you change it, it doesn't change anywhere else.

To embed an object:

- Select the information you want to embed.
- Copy it.
- Go to the document where you want the information to appear and put the insertion point where you want it.
- Choose Paste Special from the Edit menu.
- Choose Paste and the format you want to use.

Scraps

Scraps are a neat new feature in Windows 95. In programs that support OLE 2.0, you can copy and paste by dragging selections to the desktop.

- Select the text or graphic you want to copy.
- Drag it to the desktop. If you're working in a full-screen window, you'll need to click the Restore icon on the program's title bar to make the window smaller so you can see the desktop.

- Drag the selection to the desktop. It appears as a "scrap."

- Locate the program or document you want to put the scrap in and drag the scrap to its icon or open document window.

Create a scrap of your home address so you can drop it in other documents. Make scraps of anything else you use regularly, such as "boilerplate" text, or Aunt Caroline's address.

Here's How

To	Do
Display the Start menu	Press Ctrl+Esc.
Start programs	Click on the Start menu button and choose the program you want. Or double-click on its icon in My Computer or the Explorer. Or right-click on the Start button and choose Open. Or double-click its icon on the desktop or in the Find dialog box. Or click on a document you worked with in the Start menu's Documents folder. Or, in a DOS window, enter the command used to start a program. Or choose Run from the Start menu. Or drag and drop a document icon onto a program's icon or shortcut or into an open program window. Or right-click on a document and choose Open or Send To.
Put a program on the Start menu	Drag the program's icon to the Start button.
Go to the Explorer	Right-click on the Start button and choose Explore.
Start a program from the Explorer	Click in the left-hand pane of the Explorer window You'll see the folder's contents in the right pane as you open folders. When you locate the program you want to run, double-click on it.
Switch between programs	Click on its name on the taskbar. Or press Alt+Tab or Alt+Esc.

To	Do
Clean off your screen quickly	Right-click on a blank area of the taskbar and choose Minimize All Windows. To get the windows back the way they were, do the same thing and choose Undo Minimize All.
Open a document from a program	Choose Open from its File menu or click the "open folder" icon on the toolbar.
Save a document	Press Ctrl+S, choose Save from the File menu, or click the little disk icon on program's toolbar. The first time you save a document, you'll see the Save As dialog box.
Close a program window (exit)	Click the Close box in the far-right corner or press Alt+F4. Or right-click on its button on the taskbar and choose Close.
Move through a list in a dialog box	Press PgUp and PgDn, Home or End, or type the first letter in a name to go directly to that part of the list.
Sort files in an Open dialog box	View file details and click on the headings.
Rename items in an Open or Save As dialog box	Click on the name, or select it and press F2. Type the new name and press Enter.
Display names that match a pattern in Open dialogs	Use wildcards.
Open several documents at once	Ctrl-click on them in an Open dialog; then double-click on the last one. (Doesn't work in all programs.)
Move items in an Open/Save As dialog	Use Ctrl+X, Ctrl+V, or right-click and choose Cut, or drag the item to another folder.
Copy items in an Open/Save As dialog	Use Ctrl+C, Ctrl+V, or right-click and choose Copy, or Ctrl-drag the item to another folder.

To	Do
Create a shortcut in an Open/Save As dialog	Right-click on the item and choose Create Shortcut.
Delete in Open/ Save As dialogs	Select files and press Del, or right-click and choose Delete.
Print from an Open/Save As dialog	Right-click on a document's name and choose Print.
Look at file contents in an Open/Save As dialog	Right-click on a file; then choose QuickView to see what's in it.
Go to the Find utility from an Open/Save As dialog	Right-click on a folder; then choose Find.
Go to the Explorer from an Open/Save As dialog	Right-click on a folder and choose Explore.
Copy and rename files at the same time	Use the Save As command in a program.
Save a document as a different file type	Use the Save As command in a program.
Copy text that takes up more than one screen	Shift-click to select it.
Copy text or graphics in a program	Select it and press Ctrl+C. You can also right-click on it and choose Copy, or choose Copy from the program's Edit menu, or click the Copy icon on the program's toolbar. Then paste it.
Move text or graphics in a program	Select it and press Ctrl+X. You can also right-click on it and choose Cut, or choose Cut from the program's Edit menu, or click the Cut icon on the program's toolbar. Then paste it.

To	Do
Paste text or graphics in a program	Select it and press Ctrl+V. You can also right-click on it and choose Paste, or choose Paste from the program's Edit menu, or click the Paste icon on the program's toolbar.
Copy and move by dragging and dropping	Drag over what you want to select. Put the cursor inside the selection. Press the left mouse button and drag to put it in another location.
Link something from one document to another	Copy it; go to the other program and choose Paste Link from the Edit menu.
Embed something from one document into another	Copy it; go to the other program and choose Paste Special from the Edit menu.
Create a scrap	Copy a selection and drag it to the desktop.

Printing

You probably installed a printer when you installed Windows, or maybe someone else set it up for you. If you've been printing just fine with no problems, you may not even be interested in this chapter. But if you haven't installed a printer, if you've bought new fonts for your printer, or if you're having trouble printing, you may find some valuable information here. Printing's different in Windows 95.

Finding Your Printer

The first task is to find your printer. It's listed in at least three different places—on the Start menu (look in Settings and Printers) and in My Computer and the Explorer, in the Printers folder near the bottom of the folders list.

If you can't find your printer, you probably don't have one installed.

▶ **Tip:** *Once you find your printer, Ctrl-click on it and drag it to the desktop to make a shortcut you can find again.*

Installing a Printer

Use the Add Printer wizard in the Printers folder to install a printer or add new printers to your setup. Double-click the Add printer icon. When you see the Add Printer wizard, click Next. Choose a port and click Next again; then choose a printer from the list. Now follow the prompts on the screen.

The only hard part is guessing which port your printer's on. They're usually on LPT1. Try that first. You'll get a chance to print a test page; if it doesn't print, go back and change the port.

You may also need to find your printer installation disks or your Windows installation disks, which have the printer drivers on them. If Windows needs one of these disks, it'll ask you for it.

The Default Printer

When you go to print, Windows will print with the printer you've selected as the default printer. You'll be asked during the printer installation process if you want the printer you're installing to be the default printer.

> **Tip:** *If you have a portable computer, install on it a couple of printers you might come across in your travels. HP LaserJets are pretty common.*

You can install more than one printer, but only one will be the default printer at any one time.

In fact, you may want to install several printers, such as the one you have at home and the ones you have at work. That way, you can format documents exactly for a certain printer, even though it's not really attached to your computer. Most folks don't even notice, but formatting changes take place when you switch printers.

> **Tip:** *To change to a different default printer, right-click on the printer's icon and choose Set As Default.*

Printing

Once you've installed a printer, all you have to do to is drag a document's icon to the icon of your printer. If you're in a program, choose Print from its File menu, or click the tiny printer icon on its toolbar, if it has one.

> **Tip:** *Add your printer and your fax to your Send To folder, so that all you have to do to print a document is right-click on its icon and choose Send To.*

You'll see a printer icon on the taskbar, next to the clock, when a print job is in process.

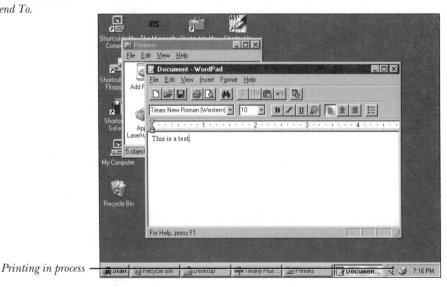

Printing in process

As you send each print job, it's placed in a queue, or lineup, and printed in the order it's received, working like a short-order cook. You can look at how the documents are lined up in this print queue and change the order they'll be printed in, if you're in a rush for a particular document.

Double-click on the printer icon on the taskbar to see the print queue. You can also double-click on the printer's button on the taskbar or the printer's icon on the desktop (if you put one there) to see the print queue.

▶ **Tip:** *Watch that printer icon. A red question mark appears on it if there's a printing problem, such as your having to insert a special sheet of paper.*

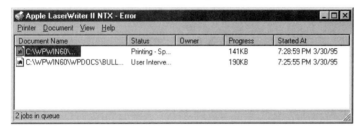

To change the printing order, just drag the icon of the document to a new location in the print queue. You can't change the order of the one that's printing, though.

If a print job's under way, you can drag documents to the printer icon on the taskbar to add them to the line of documents waiting to be printed.

Paper jam? Right-click on the printer's icon and choose Pause Printing.

Pausing Printing

To restart the printer, choose Pause Printer again so that the command's unchecked.

Stop That Job! If you decide that you'd rather not print a document that's waiting in the queue, select it by clicking on it; then click Cancel Printing.

▶ **Tip:** *Want a copy of what's on the screen? Press the Print Screen key. Then open Paint and paint Ctrl+V to paste the image. Now you can print it. Pressing Alt+Print Screen captures the active window.*

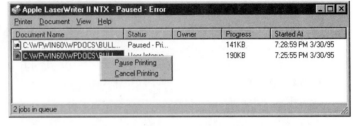

If you want to cancel printing *everything*, right-click on your printer icon and choose Purge Print Jobs. Or double-click on the printer icon on the taskbar and choose Purge Print Jobs from the Printer menu.

Using Printer Properties

You may be wondering how you adjust your printer's settings. The secret is: change the printer's properties. Right-click on the printer's icon and choose Properties. You'll see all sorts of tabs with all sorts of things you can change. Most of the time you'll leave these alone, because changing something here changes how the printer behaves every time you print. Normally you'll change things like paper size only for one or two documents, and you do that through your program's Print and Page Setup dialog boxes.

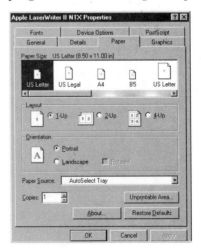

In fact, you'll find new Page Setup dialog boxes in Windows 95 programs. They have new features that you may be looking for in setting up your printer. For example, they now combine paper-handling features that used to be part of Printer Setup and let you control margin settings as well. This one's from Microsoft Word.

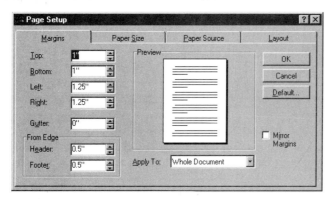

Fonts

Windows comes with a set of TrueType fonts that are automatically installed. TrueType fonts are different from other fonts you may have used. Basically, they're easier to use and take up much less room on your hard disk than other kinds of fonts, because they don't require separate versions of each font and size, one for the screen and one for the printer. They're easy to use; you can use them in just about any size; a lot of them are available, and they're inexpensive.

In a nutshell, my advice is stick with TrueType fonts if you're just starting out in Windows. You'll have a lot less to learn. You may already have other fonts, though, such as PostScript fonts or cartridge fonts (if you have a cartridge printer). Don't worry; you can still use the fonts you have, and install new ones, too.

Windows 95 keeps all its fonts in one big Fonts folder inside the Control Panel folder. If you use lots of different fonts (by which I mean fifty or so), or if you use PostScript fonts, you'll probably want to purchase a third-party Windows 95 font manager to handle creating subsets of fonts to use with different jobs. Otherwise your font lists can get *very* long.

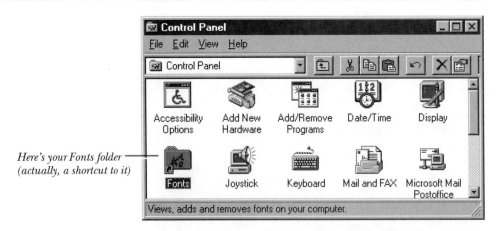

Here's your Fonts folder ────
(actually, a shortcut to it)

If you have other fonts, or if you buy fonts on disk or font cartridges, you'll need to install them.

Installing Fonts

To install fonts, you'll use the Fonts folder inside the Control Panel folder:

Click on My Computer or choose Settings from the Start menu and pick Control Panel. Then:

• Open the Fonts folder and choose Install New Font from the File menu.

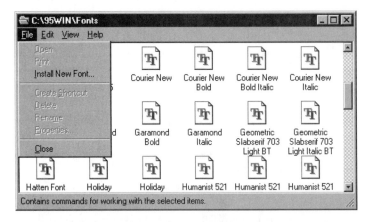

• Under Folders (see the next page), open the folder that contains the fonts you want to install. Click Drives if you're installing fonts from a floppy disk, and then choose the drive that has the disk in it.

- When you see the list of fonts, Ctrl-click on the ones you want to install, or click the Select All button to select all of them. (If you're selecting most of them, select them all and then Ctrl-click to deselect the ones you don't want; it's faster than selecting most of them individually.)

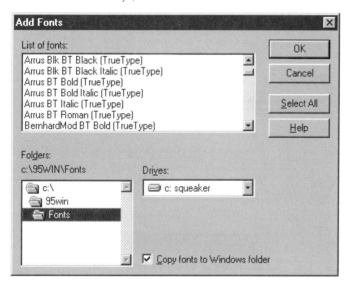

Keep the Copy Fonts to Windows Directory box checked unless you're using fonts that are shared on a network; then click OK.

You use a different procedure to install cartridge fonts. They're specific to each printer, so you use the printer's Properties sheet instead of the Fonts folder. First, install the fonts using the program that came with the cartridge. Then right-click on the printer's icon and choose Properties. Finally, go to the Fonts tab and select the cartridge fonts you want to use.

Installing Cartridge Fonts

▶ **Tip:** *Printer fonts (specific to your printer) don't appear in the Fonts folder. You'll see them in font lists in programs, though.*

Windows 95 makes it easy for you to see what a font looks like before you use it. Just double-click on a font icon in the Fonts folder, and you'll see samples of that font, all the way up to 72 points. Click Print to get a hard copy.

Previewing Fonts

You can tell TrueType from other fonts, because there's a "TT" on their icons and no point sizes are listed for them.

TrueType font ————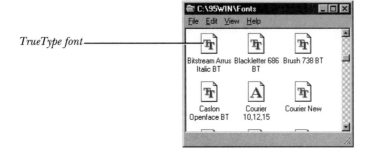

Deleting Fonts

▶ **Tip:** *Don't remove the Marlett font! Windows needs it for symbols in dialog boxes.*

To send a font you never use to the Recycle Bin, select it in the Fonts folder and press Del. However, you might delete a font and decide that you want it back again. Instead of deleting fonts, create a new folder named Old Fonts and store fonts you never use there so that you can get them back again without having to reinstall them.

Special Tools

View the Toolbar in the Fonts folder (choose Toolbar from the View menu), and you'll see a new icon, the one with the ABs on it. This new tool lets you group fonts that are similar to each other.

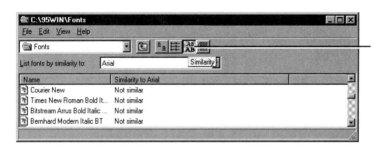

Click here to group fonts by similarity

If you're trying to decide which font to use out of a huge list of fonts in the Fonts folder, this little trick can save you some time.

Another thing you can do to manage a big Fonts folder is hide variations (bold, italics, and so forth) so that there aren't so many icons to choose from. Instead of seeing separate icons for Arial, Arial Black, Arial Bold, Arial Bold Italic, Arial Italic, ad infinitum, you'll see just one icon for Arial. Choose this handy command from the View menu.

One Last Font Trick

This one can drive you nuts unless you know what's happening.

When a PostScript printer gets a request for a TrueType font such as Times New Roman or Arial, it usually substitutes its equivalent built-in fonts, named Times and Helvetica. You won't get the TrueType font that's displayed on the screen; instead you'll be getting PostScript fonts in your printed document. They're very close, but not exactly alike.

To fix this, go to the printer's property sheet and click the Fonts tab. Then click Always Use TrueType fonts.

Special Characters

Almost all fonts have hidden special characters. Use the Character Map accessory shown on the next page to see what these are. It's in the Programs folder inside the Accessories folder. Choose a font from its Font list, and you'll see the characters available in that font.

To insert a special character, just double-click on it. You can copy several characters without closing the window. Then click Copy, go to the document where you want the symbols, and paste.

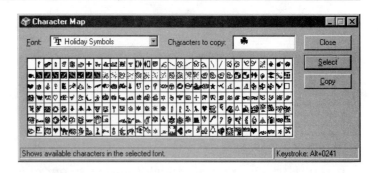

Troubleshooting Printing Problems

Sometimes things don't always work as you'd like them to, especially printing. Trouble always seems to happen more frequently than most of us would like. If your printer won't print, here are a few things to check for, more or less in order of difficulty.

Check to see that the printer's on. Check that it has paper. See if the cables are tightly connected. Run its self-test.

▶ **Tip:** *Use the Printer Troubleshooting wizard if you have trouble printing! In Help, click the Contents tab; then double-click on Troubleshooting and If You Have Trouble Printing.*

Check the print queue by double-clicking on the printer icon on the taskbar next to the clock. See if there are any messages in the print queue about what may be going wrong. (If no printer icon's there, nothing's being printed.) Check that the printer that's selected is the one you're trying to print with. Try deleting all the print jobs except one.

Try printing from WordPad, the accessory that comes with Windows 95. If you can print from there, the problem is probably in the program you're trying to print from, not in Windows. Check the Printer Setup dialog box in your program and make sure you're on the right printer.

If all else fails, install your printer again. The driver may have become corrupted. You'll need the original Windows 95 installation disks or the disk that came with your printer, if you have one.

Don't forget the Printer Troubleshooting wizard. And if worst comes to worst, get out your printer manual.

Here's How

To	Do
Find your printer	Look in Settings and Printers on the Start menu and in My Computer and the Explorer, in the Printers folder near the bottom of the folders list.
Add a new printer	Use the Add Printer wizard in the Printers folder in the Control Panels folder.
Change to a different default printer	Right-click on the printer's icon and choose Set As Default.
Print a document	Drag a document's icon to the icon of your printer. Or if you're already printing, drag documents to the printer icon on the taskbar to add them to the line of documents waiting to be printed. If you're in a program, choose Print from its File menu, or click the tiny printer icon on its toolbar, if it has one.
See the print queue	Double-click on the printer icon on the taskbar. Or double-click on the printer's icon on the desktop (if you put one there).
Change the printing order	Drag a document to a new location in the print queue.
Pause the printer	Right-click on the printer's icon and choose Pause Printing.
Restart the printer	Choose Pause Printer again so that the command's unchecked.
Print what's on the screen	Press the Print Screen key. Then open Paint and press Ctrl+V to paste the image. Pressing Alt+Print Screen captures the active window.
Stop a document from printing	Select it in the print queue; then click Cancel Printing.

To	Do
Cancel printing everything	Right-click on your printer icon and choose Purge Print Jobs. Or double-click on the printer icon on the taskbar and choose Purge Print Jobs from the Printer menu.
Change the printer's properties	Right-click on the printer's icon and choose Properties.
Install fonts	Double-click on the Fonts folder inside the Control Panel folder. Choose Install New Fonts from the File menu.
Install cartridge fonts	Install the fonts using the program that came with the cartridge. Right-click on the printer's icon and choose Properties. Go to the Fonts tab and select the cartridge fonts you want to use.
See samples of a font	Double-click on its icon in the Fonts folder.
Delete a font	Select it in the Fonts folder and press Del.
Use a font's special characters	Use the Character Map accessory in the Accessories folder inside the Programs folder.

It's not You; It's...

Something always goes wrong, sooner or later. But it's not you. It's something wrong in your computer system. And somewhere there's a solution to almost any problem.

Windows 95 comes with a set of troubleshooting Wizards that can hold your hand through all sorts of common problems. The Wizards reside in the Help system. Press F1, click the Contents tab, and double-click on the Troubleshooting icon. Then see if any of those questions look like what you're having trouble with. If so, double-click on the question mark icon next to the topic, and you'll be taken through troubleshooting procedures step by step.

▶ **Tip:** *Another way to find a troubleshooting Wizard quickly: Once you're in the Help system, click the Find tab. Enter a word that describes your problem, such as* **memory;** *then double-click on Memory troubleshooter. Follow the instructions on the screen.*

Then, on the other hand, maybe it's one of these problems....

Where are the games? If you discover that you're missing some components (like the games! or Briefcase), go to the Add/Remove Programs control panel and click the Windows Setup tab. You'll see what's been installed and what hasn't. Check an item's box to install it if it's not there. Click OK. You'll be asked for the installation disks, so have them or the CD-ROM handy.

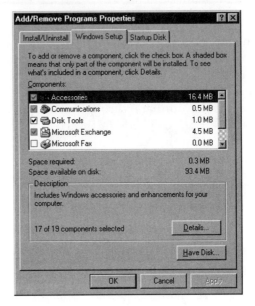

Why won't the computer start? Windows 95 comes ready to create an emergency startup disk for you that can jump-start your computer if it isn't starting normally from the hard drive and can diagnose what may be wrong. Needless to say, it's best to make this emergency startup disk before the computer won't start. Perhaps you might do it now, if you didn't do it when Windows was installed.

• Find your Windows 95 installation disks or the CD-ROM; you'll be asked for them as you follow the instructions on the screen.

- Go to the Control Panel and double-click on Add/Remove Programs.
- Click the Startup Disk tab.
- Click Create Disk.
- Get yourself a high-density blank disk or one that has stuff on it that you don't want any more and put it in drive A.

To use the startup disk, put it in drive A and turn on your computer. You'll wind up at the A: prompt. Try the easiest solution first. Enter **scandisk c: /autofix.**

If that doesn't fix the problem, you'll need to know a bit about computers. That startup disk contains Sys.com. Drvspace.bin, Msd.exe, Fdisk.exe, Edit.com, Format.com, Attrib.exe, and maybe some more useful stuff. If these things sound familiar to you, go ahead and use them. If not, you'll be better off calling for help.

Windows isn't running right! Try starting Windows in "safe" mode. This means that Windows 95 uses just the bare-bones settings—no printers, CD-ROM drives, and so forth, just enough to start. To start in safe mode, turn your computer off. (Choose Shut Down from the Start menu if you can, but maybe you can't if Windows isn't running right.) Turn it back on again. Press F8 when you hear the beep or see "Starting Windows 95". Choose option 3 to start Windows on a standalone computer or option 4 to start with a network connection. Once you get it started, you can go to the Control Panel folder and adjust settings there, or use one of the many Troubleshooting Wizards to analyze the problem.

Out of disk space? Here's the quick way to see how much disk space you have left.

Just double-click My Computer; then right-click on the disk you want to check. Finally, choose Properties.

Need to free disk space? Did you forget to empty the Recycle Bin? It has all the files you deleted.

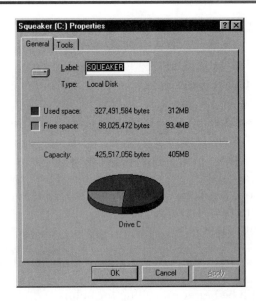

If the Recycle Bin's empty, you can delete other things to free disk space:

- Delete files you don't need any more. Go to the Explorer and view them with details. Click on the Modified column to see the oldest files first. Move old data files you don't need to floppy disks. Be careful not to move files that programs need, even if they're old. Move only files you created yourself.

- Delete entire programs that you don't use any more.

- Remember to empty the Recycle Bin this time.

- Delete Windows components that you never use (double-click the Add/Remove Programs icon in the Control Panel folder) and then remove things you never use. You can save a whopping 14 Mb just by deleting the Accessories.

Some device not working? Use the System icon in the Control Panel folder to check out what Windows thinks you have attached to your system. Click the Device Manager tab; then click on the little plus signs to see each device, such as your floppy drives, CD-ROM, or whatever.

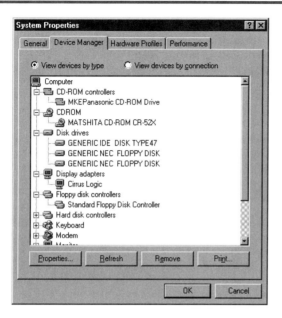

Any devices that aren't working will have a "No Way" red icon over them. Double-click on that icon to see a message about what's wrong.

I'm out of memory! If you frequently get messages saying you're out of memory, the basic problem is that you need to buy more RAM. Windows 95 likes lots of it. It especially likes 12 Mb or so. But in the meantime, here's what you can do.

- Quit any programs you don't need.

- Close any windows you aren't using. There may be more windows open than the taskbar can display. Look for a tiny icon that looks like a filing cabinet. It indicates that there are more windows open than those that are showing. Close them.

- If you're still getting the message, quit everything and restart your computer.

If you're *still* getting the message, run the "If you run out of memory" troubleshooting Wizard.

That should do it, at least until you can get down to Memory R Us for more memory.

▶ **Tip:** *If you don't see the red light, to check system resources, double-click the System icon in the Control Panels folder; then click the Performance tab.*

Resource red light? There's a resource monitor on the taskbar. It turns red, like an idiot light on your dashboard, when you get low on resources. If it turns red on you, quit any programs you don't need. Close any windows you aren't using. If that doesn't do it, quit everything and restart your computer.

Missing something from the Start menu? All of a sudden something that was on your Start menu isn't there any more! There's a way to rebuild your program folders.

Click the Start button and select the Run command. In the command line box, enter GRPCONV /S.

This is the equivalent to running SETUP /P in Win3.1, which restored your program groups.

Finally, run Scandisk on your hard drive to make sure the missing-group problem wasn't caused by a problem with your disk.

Mouse pointer jumping? The simplest reason for this phenomenon is that its moving part (I hate to say "mouse ball") needs to be cleaned. The second most common reason is that you need to change its tracking speed in the Mouse control panel. Click the Motion tab. If you're getting something *really* weird on the screen, you may have checked Show pointer trails by mistake

Mouse not working? If your mouse doesn't work, you can still do basic operations in Windows until you figure out what the problem is. To use the keyboard instead of the mouse when you're at the desktop:

▶ **Tip:** *Press Alt+F4 to close programs and dialog boxes.*

- Press Ctrl+Esc to go to the start button with the menu opened. (Then, typing **u** shuts Windows down.)
- Press Esc to get just the Start button selected (unopened).
- Press Alt+Tab to get to an open program or folder.
- Press the arrow keys to go between icons in a window. Press Enter to open a selected icon.

Look in Appendix A for more keyboard equivalents.

Coming down with a virus? If your computer suddenly slows down or you start seeing error messages that you've never seen before, you may have a virus. The first thing to do is *turn off your computer.* Then restart it from that emergency floppy disk that you had the foresight to make. Before you put it in drive A, write-protect that disk so that it won't get infected, too. (Open the hole of a 3.5-inch disk; cover the tab of a 5.25-inch disk.)

Now start your computer from the bootable floppy. Put it in drive A and turn the computer on. Then use an antivirus program and scan your hard disk. Almost all antivirus programs have options that will repair your infected files, or at least identify them so you can delete them.

Don't stop after your hard disk is working again! Scan *all* your floppies, starting with the ones you used most recently. They may have the virus on them. If you have a tape backup, it could be infected, too. Restore it onto your hard disk and scan those files, or reformat your backup tape so that you won't be tempted to restore from it.

Still stuck? Call Microsoft Product Support at (206) 637-7089, although this phone number may have been replaced by a special Windows 95 number by the time you read this. Use (206) 882-8080 to get the main switchboard. Before you call, make sure you have a pretty good idea of what your system is—what kind of hardware you have, the exact name of the folder where Windows is installed, what kind of mouse you're using, what video display you've got, and so forth. You may need to find the manuals. But if you can get to the DOS prompt, run the MSD (Microsoft Support Diagnostics) program. It will tell you all these things. Print its report and have it handy before you call. It may also be helpful, depending on what you're running, to print out a copy of your AUTOEXEC.BAT and CONFIG.SYS files, because whoever answers the phone at Microsoft will probably ask you what's in them.

Good luck! Maybe you'll never have to call!

Here's How

To	Do
Add a new printer	Use the Add Printer wizard in the Printers folder in the Control Panels folder.
Arrange windows	Right-click on a blank spot on the taskbar; then choose Cascade or Tile Horizontally or Tile Vertically.
Bring up the Start menu	Press Ctrl+Esc.
Bypass the Recycle Bin	Press Shift+Del.
Cancel printing everything	Right-click on your printer icon and choose Purge Print Jobs. Or double-click on the printer icon on the taskbar and choose Purge Print Jobs from the Printer menu.
Cascade windows	Right-click on the taskbar and choose Cascade.
Change a shortcut's icon	Right-click on a shortcut icon and choose Properties. Then click the Shortcut tab and the Change icon button.
Change the date and time	Double-click on the time on the taskbar.
Change the date and time formats	Double-click on the Control Panels folder's Regional Settings icon and click the Time and the Date tabs.

To	Do
Change the desktop pattern's color	Right-click on the desktop; then choose Properties from the pop-up menu that appears. Click the desktop property sheet's Appearance tab.
Change the desktop's pattern and wallpaper	Right-click on the desktop; then choose Properties from the pop-up menu that appears. Click the Background tab.
Change the mouse from right-handed to left-handed	Choose Settings from the Start menu and click Control Panel. Double-click on the Mouse icon. Click the Buttons tab.
Change the pointer's speed	Choose Settings from the Start menu and click Control Panel. Double-click on the Mouse icon. Click the Motion tab.
Change the printer's properties	Right-click on the printer's icon and choose Properties.
Change the printing order	Drag a document to a new location in the print queue.
Change the screen font	Right-click on the desktop; then choose Properties from the pop-up menu that appears. In the desktop property sheet's Appearance tab, pick a different font.
Change the size of the Explorer's panes	Drag the bar between the two windows.
Change the system sounds	Choose Settings from the Start menu and click Control Panel. Double-click on the Sounds icon.
Change the taskbar's properties	Right-click on the taskbar and choose Properties.
Change the whole color scheme	Right-click on the desktop; then choose Properties from the pop-up menu that appears. Click the desktop property sheet's Appearance tab; then, under Scheme, click the downward-pointing arrow to see a list of preset schemes.

To	Do
Change to a different default printer	Right-click on the printer's icon and choose Set As Default.
Choose a command button	Click on it or press Enter.
Choose a screen saver	Right-click on the desktop; then choose Properties from the pop-up menu that appears. Click the desktop property sheet's Screen Saver tab.
Choose an item in a dialog box	Click on the selection, or type Alt-*letter* (where *letter* is the letter in the box).
Choose an option button or check box	Click on it or move to it and press the space bar.
Choose several items in a list (sometimes)	Ctrl-click on them.
Clean off your screen quickly	Right-click on a blank area of the taskbar and choose Minimize All Windows. To get the windows back the way they were, do the same thing and choose Undo Minimize All.
Close a folder and all its containing folders	Shift-click on a folder window's Close button.
Close a program window	Click the Close box in the far-right corner or press Alt+F4. Or right-click on its button on the taskbar and choose Close.
Close a window	Double-click on its System icon, click its Close box, or press Alt-F4.
Collapse the tree in the Explorer's left pane	Double-click on the Desktop icon at the beginning of the list of folders in the left-hand window. Or use the - on the numeric keypad.
Copy items in an Open/Save As dialog	Use Ctrl+C, Ctrl+V, or right-click and choose Copy, or Ctrl-drag the item to another folder.

To	Do
Copy to another drive	Drag or press Ctrl+C, Ctrl+V.
Copy to another folder on the same drive	Ctrl-drag or press Ctrl+C, Ctrl+V.
Copy a floppy disk	Right-click on the icon of the floppy disk drive you want to use and choose Copy Disk.
Copy and move by dragging and dropping	Drag over what you want to select. Put the cursor inside the selection. Press the left mouse button and drag to put it in another location.
Copy and rename files at the same time	Use the Save As command in a program.
Copy files onto a floppy disk	Drag them to the icon of the floppy disk drive, or right-click on them and choose Send To.
Copy text or graphics in a program	Select it and press Ctrl+C. You can also right-click on it and choose Copy, or choose Copy from the program's Edit menu, or click the Copy icon on the program's toolbar. Then paste it.
Copy text that takes up more than one screen	Shift-click to select it.
Create a custom pattern	Right-click on the desktop; then choose Properties from the pop-up menu that appears. In the desktop property sheet's Background tab, click the Edit Pattern button.
Create a new folder	Right-click in a My Computer or Explorer window and choose New; then choose Folder.
Create a scrap	Copy a selection and drag it to the desktop.
Create a shortcut	Drag a program's icon (or Ctrl-drag anything else) to the desktop. Choose Create Shortcut here.

To	Do
Create a shortcut to your floppy drives	Click in the Explorer's left pane and press Home, or open My Computer. Drag your floppy drive icons to the desktop.
Create a shortcut in an Open/Save As dialog	Right-click on the item and choose Create Shortcut.
Customize the key repeat rate	Double-click on the Keyboard icon in the Control Panels folder. Move the Repeat rate slider bar.
Delete a font	Select it in the Fonts folder and press Del.
Delete an icon	Select it and press Del. Then empty the Recycle Bin.
Delete in Open/Save As dialogs	Select files and press Del, or right-click and choose Delete.
Deselect all but one file	Click on that file.
Deselect everything	Click somewhere else, or press Ctrl+Z.
Deselect one file	Ctrl-click on it.
Display names that match a pattern in Open dialogs	Use wildcards.
Display the Start menu	Press Ctrl+Esc.
Embed something from one document into another	Copy it; go to the other program and choose Paste Special from the Edit menu.
Erase a used disk	Right-click on the icon of the floppy disk drive or its shortcut. Choose Format. Click the Quick button.
Exit from Windows	Click the Start button and choose Shut Down.
Expand the tree in the Explorer's left pane	Double-click on the Desktop icon in the list, or select the drive and press the + on the numeric keypad.

To	Do
Find a file or folder	Choose Find from the Tools menu, choose Files or Folders, and enter a file or folder's name. Make sure the Look in box displays the name of your hard drive if you want to search the whole drive. Click Find Now.
Find your printer	Look in Settings and Printers on the Start menu and in My Computer and the Explorer, in the Printers folder near the bottom of the folders list.
Format a floppy disk	Right-click on the icon of the floppy disk drive or its shortcut. Choose Format.
Get help	Click on Help on the menu bar, press Alt-H, or press F1. If you see a question mark in a dialog box, click on it and then move the pointer to the item you need help about.
Go to the Explorer	Right-click on the Start button and choose Explore.
Go to the Explorer from an Open/ Save As dialog	Right-click on a folder and choose Explore.
Go to the Find utility from an Open/ Save As dialog	Right-click on a folder; then choose Find.
Go to a folder	Choose Go To from the Explorer's Tools menu, type in the path to the folder or file you want to go to, and click OK.
Go to a folder you went to	Click on the downward-pointing arrow next to the text box in the Go To Folder dialog box.
Go to My Computer	Double-click its icon on your desktop.
Go to the bottom of a My Computer/Explorer list or window	Press End.

To	Do
Go to the top of a My Computer/Explorer list or window	Press Home.
Go up one level in My Computer or the Explorer	Press Backspace.
Install cartridge fonts	Install the fonts using the program that came with the cartridge. Right-click on the printer's icon and choose Properties. Go to the Fonts tab and select the cartridge fonts you want to use.
Install fonts	Double-click on the Fonts folder inside the Control Panel folder. Choose Install New Fonts from the File menu.
Keep Help on top	When you're looking at a Help topic, click its Options button and choose Keep Help on Top; then click On Top.
Link something from one document to another	Copy it; go to the other program and choose Paste Link from the Edit menu.
Look at file contents in an Open/Save As dialog	Right-click on a file; then choose QuickView to see what's in it.
Look at the contents of a folder	Click on a folder in the Explorer's left pane, or double-click on a folder in My Computer.
Make the Help text bigger	Right-click inside a Help topic; then choose Font.
Maximize a window	Double-click in its title bar or click its Maximize icon.
Minimize a window	Click its Minimize icon.

To	Do
Mix your own colors	Right-click on the desktop; then choose Properties from the pop-up menu that appears. In the desktop property sheet's Appearance tab, click in the Color box and then click Other at the bottom of the color palette.
Move items in an Open/Save As dialog	Use Ctrl+X, Ctrl+V, or right-click and choose Cut, or drag the item to another folder.
Movea file to another drive	Ctrl-drag or press Ctrl+X, Ctrl+V.
Move a file to another folder on the same drive	Drag or press Ctrl+X, Ctrl+V.
Move folders to other locations	Drag them in the Explorer's left pane, or cut and paste.
Move the taskbar	Drag it.
Move text or graphics in a program	Select it and press Ctrl+X. You can also right-click on it and choose Cut, or choose Cut from the program's Edit menu, or click the Cut icon on the program's toolbar Then paste it.
Move a window	Drag it by its title bar.
Move through a window	Drag or click in the scroll bars, or click on the arrow icons. Or press Pgup and PgDn.
Move through a list in a dialog box	Press PgUp and PgDn, Home or End, or type the first letter in a name to go directly to that part of the list.
Move within a dialog box	Click in it, or press Tab to move forward or Shift-Tab to move backward.
Name your computer	Double-click My Computer. Right-click drive C or whatever your hard drive is. Choose Properties and click the General tab. Type a new label for your hard drive.

To	Do
Open or close a folder in the Explorer's left pane	Click on it, or press the + and - keys on the numeric keypad when the folder's selected.
Open a document from a program	Choose Open from its File menu or click the "open folder" icon on the toolbar.
Open multiple folders in the Explorer	Ctrl-click on folders in the right-hand pane and then Ctrl-double-click on the last one. Or open multiple copies of the Explorer by double-clicking on its icon.
Open several documents at once	Ctrl-click on them in an Open dialog; then double-click on the last one.
Open a window	Double-click on its icon or press Enter when the icon is highlighted.
Paste text or graphics in a program	Select it and press Ctrl+V. You can also right-click on it and choose Paste, or choose Paste from the program's Edit menu, or click the Paste icon on the program's toolbar.
Pause the printer	Right-click on the printer's icon and choose Pause Printing.
Print a document	Drag a document's icon to the icon of your printer. Or if you're already printing, drag documents to the printer icon on the taskbar to add them to the line of documents waiting to be printed. If you're in a program, choose Print from its File menu, or click the tiny printer icon on its toolbar, if it has one.
Print from an Open/ Save As dialog	Right-click on a document's name and choose Print.
Print what's on the screen	Press the Print Screen key. Then open Paint and press Ctrl+V to paste the image. Press Alt+Print Screen to capture the active window.

To	Do
Put something on the Start menu	Drag its icon to the Start menu button.
Rename a file or folder	Click on its name and retype the new name, or press F2.
Rename items in an Open or Save As dialog box	Click on the name, or select it and press F2. Type the new name and press Enter.
Restart the printer	Right-click on the printer's icon and choose Pause Printer again so that the command's unchecked.
Restore a window	Double-click in its title bar or click its Restore icon.
Save a document	Press Ctrl+S, choose Save from the File menu, or click the little disk icon on program's toolbar. The first time you save a document, you'll see the Save As dialog box.
Save a document as a different file type	Use the Save As command in a program.
Scroll a list in a dialog box	Click on the up or down arrow in the scroll box, click within the scroll box itself, or type Alt-*letter* and then press the down arrow key.
See the files you worked with most recently	Click on the Modified button when you're viewing details.
See folders that are inside a folder	Click on the + next to a folder in the Explorer's left pane, or double-click on a folder in the right pane. In My Computer, double-click on a folder.
See the print queue	Double-click on the printer icon on the taskbar. Or double-click on the printer's icon on the desktop (if you put one there).
See samples of a font	Double-click on its icon in the Fonts folder.

To	Do
See the structure of your computer at a glance	Click on the down arrow next to whatever's listed at the top of the left-hand pane in My Computer and the Explorer.
See what's on your computer	Go to My Computer or the Explorer.
Select adjacent items	Press Shift, click on the first one, and then click on the last one. Or drag over them: Click at the top-left corner of the group; then drag to the bottom-right corner.
Select all the files in a window or list	Press Ctrl+A.
Select an item (an icon or an item in a list)	Click on it.
Select from menus	Click on the item or press Alt and type the underlined letter or number. When the menu appears, click on the item, or type the underlined letter or number. You can also highlight the name with the arrow keys and press Enter, or use a keyboard shortcut if one is available.
Select more than one item	Press Ctrl and click on each one.
Set up your mouse	Choose Settings from the Start menu and click Control Panel. Double-click on the Mouse icon.
Size a window	Drag it outward or inward by its corner.
Sort files	View file details and click on the headings.
Start a program automatically	Put a shortcut to it in your Startup folder (in your Windows directory in the Start menu folder).

To	Do
Start programs	Click on the Start menu button and choose the program you want. Or double-click on its icon in My Computer or the Explorer. Or right-click on the Start button and choose Open. Or double-click its icon on the desktop or in the Find dialog box. Or click on a document you worked with in the Start menu's Documents folder. Or enter the command used to start a program from a DOS window. Or choose Run from the Start menu. Or drag and drop a document icon onto a program's icon or shortcut or into an open program window. Or right-click on a document icon and choose Open or Send To.
Start a program from the Explorer	Click in the left-hand pane of the Explorer window. You'll see the folder's contents in the right pane as you open folders. When you locate the program you want to run, double-click on it.
Start Windows 95	Turn on your computer. (Press F4 or F8 for an interactive start.)
Stop a document from printing	Select it in the print queue; then click Cancel Printing.
Switch between programs	Click on its name on the taskbar. Or press Alt+Tab or Alt+Esc.
Switch between windows	Click in the window, or click its name on the taskbar. Or press Alt+Esc or Alt+Tab.
Tile windows	Right-click on the taskbar and choose Tile Horizontally or Tile Vertically.
Turn off the sound	Click on the little speaker icon next to the time on the taskbar.
Use a font's special characters	Use the Character Map accessory in the Accessories folder inside the Programs folder.
Undo what you did	Press Ctrl+Z.

To	Do
View file details that are often necessary	Choose Options from the View menu and *uncheck* the Hide MS-DOS files extensions box. *Check* the Display full MS-DOS path in the title bar. Click OK.
View file details	Click the Details icon on the toolbar in My Computer and the Explorer.
View files before folders	Click the Name button when you're viewing details in My computer and the Explorer.
View toolbars and status bars	Choose Toolbar and Status bar from the View menu in My Computer and the Explorer.

Keyboard Shortcuts

To	Use
General	
Get help	F1
Open a file	Enter
Bring up the Start menu	Ctrl-Esc
Move to another selection, same window	Tab and Arrow keys
Move to the menu bar	F10
Choose a menu command	Alt+underlined letter
Choose a highlighted item from a menu	Enter
Cancel a menu	Esc
Cancel several cascading menus	Alt
Move between menus	Arrow keys
Open and close a System menu	Alt+Space bar
Switch between open windows (shows you a box in midscreen)	Alt+Tab

To	Use
Exit Windows (from the desktop)	Alt+F4
Quit a program	Alt+F4
Find a file or folder	F3
View the shortcut menu for a selected item	Shift+F10
Rename a file or folder	F2
Delete	Del
Delete, bypassing the Recycle Bin	Shift+Del
Copy	Ctrl+C
Cut	Ctrl+X
Paste	Ctrl+V
View an item's properties	Alt+Enter or Alt-double-click
Create a shortcut	Ctrl-Shift-drag

In My Computer and the Explorer

Refresh a window	F5
Go to	Ctrl+G
Undo	Ctrl+Z
Select All	Ctrl+A
Go up one level	Backspace
Close a folder and its enclosing folders	Shift-click on Close

To	Use
In Explorer	
Switch between panes	F6
Expand all subfolders	* on numeric keypad
Expand a folder	+ on numeric keypad
Collapse a folder	on numeric keypad
In property dialog boxes	
Move through tabs	Ctrl+Tab or Ctrl+Shift+Tab
In Open and Save As dialog boxes	
Open the Look in or Save As list	F4
Refresh the window	F5
Go up one level	Backspace
In most dialog boxes	
Move between selections	Tab or Shift-Tab
Move to a selection	Alt plus underlined letter
Move to the first or last item in a list	Home or End
Open a drop-down list box	Alt-Down arrow
Select an item in a list box	Space bar
Select a check box	Space bar
Select a command button	Enter
Close the box	Alt-F4
Close the box without selecting	Esc

Index

This Little Windows 95 Book
includes custom Little Book Fonts as well as
ITC New Baskerville and Futura Book.
It was designed by
Olav Martin Kvern,
based on an original design by
Robin Williams.

Matt S. Kim
did page makeup
in Aldus PageMaker (thank you, Matt!).